MW00380802

ENDORSEMENTS

A statement in the first chapter of Hank Kunneman's new book, *Throne Room Prophecy: Your Guide to Accurately Discerning the Word of the Lord*, really got my attention. He said, "Those who have been in the Throne Room speak words that carry the sound and weight of Heaven." As one who has been permitted to stand in the office of the prophet for 43 years, I would have loved to have had this book at the beginning of my calling! But I'm just as thrilled to have it available to me now—especially the chapter which defines the characteristics of, and differences between false prophets and true prophets. The whole Body of Christ needs to spend extra time in Chapter 6.

We all know Hank Kunneman is more than qualified to write this book. I wholeheartedly recommend it!

JESUS IS LORD!

KENNETH COPELAND

We, in God's Kingdom, have been given access! Many Christians never understand how to enter into the Father's Throne Room. Hank Kunneman's book, *Throne Room Prophecy*, is not only a tremendous teaching tool, but an example of going in before the Face of God and gaining revelation. Hank is a wonderful apostolic prophet who understands where he is seated in the heavenlies and how to enter in and know the One who has seated him for triumph here in the earth realm. The revelation he gives on the Seven Lamps of Fire, Seven Horns, and

Seven Eyes is key to bringing an understanding of a spiritual dimension that will help you walk in breakthrough today. Hank also explains what being a true prophet is like. *Throne Room Prophecy* is a must if you are called to communicate to the earth what is in the storehouse of heaven.

CHUCK PIERCE
Glory of Zion Int'l Ministries (GZI)
Global Spheres, Inc. (GSI)

God is raising up a new generation of prophets and non-prophetic people who need to understand true biblical prophecy. Your life depends on it!

SID ROTH
Host, *It's Supernatural! Television*

Perhaps the reason the Body of Christ has had such difficulty recognizing true prophets of God is because we have seen so few of them. Of course, not everyone who calls himself or herself a prophet can claim that distinction. Hank Kunneman knows what characteristics are required of those who are truly prophets sent from God, and who walk in that anointing. He has accepted the call to genuine prophetic ministry with humility. He bears the privilege of fulfilling that office and the responsibilities that accompany it with impeccable integrity. His book, *Throne Room Prophecy*, is a comprehensive and scripturally correct guide to the proper recognition and understanding of the prophetic ministry today. I am proud to recommend it to you.

DR. ROD PARSLEY
Pastor and Founder, World Harvest Church
Columbus, Ohio

In times of crisis, we need prophetic voices who speak truth in love to give us direction and hope. Hank Kunneman is one of those voices. Whether you have the gift of prophecy or want to learn more about it, Hank's biblical admonitions will encourage you to tune your heart to God's word, reminding you of the unshakable truth of the gospel in a time of great uncertainty.

SAMUEL RODRIGUEZ
New Season Lead Pastor
NHCLC President
Author of *You Are Next!*
Executive Producer of the movie *Breakthrough*

We who find ourselves longing for a double portion of God's Spirit as Elisha did, are heirs to the prophetic realm. To carry on the work in fields white for harvest as God's prophetic frontiersmen, we must better understand the prophetic ministry. In his latest book, *Throne Room Prophecy,* Pastor Hank Kunneman carefully examines the role of the prophet and the intimacy needed in order to be used in the prophetic realm. Prophecy, like other ministries contains four key characteristics: a determination to set things right that are wrong; a denouncing of evil; a love for God which causes them to speak truth, and a longing for God's people to be intimately closer to their Lord and removed from their sin. If you are looking to better understand God's divine guidance through the role of the prophetic, then this is a book for you.

MARCUS D. LAMB
Founder—President
Daystar Television Network

Finally, a book that not only discusses the prophetic but gives instruction for those who operate in this gift. In *Throne Room Prophecy,* Hank Kunneman reveals the balanced approach to the prophetic using the Word of God and his own experiences. This is a book for every Spirit-filled believer who has questioned the validity and effectiveness of prophecy. We applaud Hank Kunneman for this excellent resource.

JONI LAMB
Founder
Daystar Television Network

I have known Prophet Hank Kunneman for more than 15 years. The most impressive thing about his ministry is the purity, accuracy, and depth of his prophetic messages. In *Throne Room Prophecy* he shares principles that will help both growing prophets and people who are simply attempting to use prophetic utterances in scriptural ways. With this book as a road map, I see people using prophecy as one of the guides to national reformation, local church transformation, family development, and personal growth. The work is so profound that it could have been named "Prophecy 3.0, a new way to walk successfully with God."

BISHOP HARRY JACKSON
Senior Pastor of Hope Christian Church
Beltsville, MD

I first met Hank Kunneman in 2007. He came into my life at a time when I was facing a great challenge. His prophetic ministry both touched and changed my life. In our world today, sometimes the prophetic is misused and abused. But that is not the case in Hank's ministry. My father, Oral Roberts, called him the most accurate prophet he ever met. I have found that statement to be true. Hank's new book *Throne Room Prophecy* will give you Bible insight to the true prophetic. Read every word. I promise you, you will be blessed.

RICHARD ROBERTS
Chairman and CEO
Oral Roberts Evangelistic Association

Over many years, I have read a lot of books on the subject of prophetic ministry. Generally, most of them failed to address important issues surrounding this topic. But Hank Kunneman's *Throne Room Prophecy* hits all the issues straightforwardly. After he himself witnessed a lot of misuse, abuse, and misunderstanding in prophetic ministry over the years, he gained the wisdom needed to articulate a balanced approach to this subject. In his book, Hank addresses common misunderstandings about prophets—and there are many—along with what prophets are called to do and what they are not called to do. We live in a day when many people are calling themselves prophets, so we need to know what the Bible says on this important topic. Hank has written the book to answer most of the questions people have and to put them on a solid foundation. If you want to know more about true prophetic ministry, I encourage you to read this well-thought-out book!

RICK RENNER
Author, Teacher, Pastor, Broadcaster
Moscow, Russia

Prophetic ministry is simultaneously, credibly creative and misunderstood. Hank Kunneman has unraveled decades of prophetic experience into an understandable format that will bring clarity to this mystical gift. Those who prophesy from a throne room experience not only exhort, encourage, and edify, but also create and move mountains. This book will stir and activate the prophetic gifts in believers and give special insight for those called to prophetic ministry.

BISHOP MICHAEL PITTS
Cornerstone Global Network
MichaelPitts.com

Hank Kunneman's close connection with the Father and his consistency in prophecy has earned a high level of respect in the prophetic community and throughout the Body of Christ. Hank is indeed a rare man of God.

I love that *Throne Room Prophecy* begins with the foundation of intimacy with God himself. Words come and go; some we remember and some we forget. This intimacy with God must be the rock of every believer's walk or shipwreck is imminent. Leonard Ravenhill's quote sums this up entirely: "A man who is intimate with God is not intimidated by man."

This book is packed with so much good and practical guidance when it comes to prophecy. The information in Chapter 6 on false prophets should be required reading for every believer! Get your highlighter, notepad, laptop, or cell phone. You're going to want to make notes to review over and over from within the rich resources contained within this book!

GENE BAILEY
Senior Executive Pastor of Eagle Mountain Church and
Host of *Revival Radio TV*

My wife and I have personally witnessed the accuracy of Pastor Hank's prophetic gifting in our own lives, as well as in our church. Because he has pursued God's heart without self-promotion and has honored the One Who sits on the Throne, this accuracy speaks to his character and flows through him as God's prophetic vessel.

It's no coincidence that *Throne Room Prophecy* emerges now— during a prophetic movement in human history – to clearly convey God the Father's heart of love toward us, which is true prophetic ministry. Authentic faith, as presented by Pastor Hank in this book, is needed to hear, agree with, and speak God's goodness in our current world.

BISHOP OWEN MCMANUS, JR.
City Church of New Orleans

THRONE ROOM

Prophecy

DESTINY IMAGE BOOKS BY HANK KUNNEMAN

My Heart Cries Abba

The Prayer from the Crypt

Barrier Breakers

Spiritual A.D.D.

THRONE ROOM

Prophecy

YOUR GUIDE TO ACCURATELY
DISCERNING THE WORD OF THE LORD

HANK KUNNEMAN

DESTINY IMAGE® PUBLISHERS, INC.

P.O. Box 310, Shippensburg, PA 17257-0310

"Promoting Inspired Lives."

This book and all other Destiny Image and Destiny Image Fiction books are available at Christian bookstores and distributors worldwide.

Cover design by Eileen Rockwell
Interior design by Terry Clifton

For more information on foreign distributors, call 717-532-3040.

Reach us on the Internet: www.destinyimage.com.

ISBN 13 TP: 978-0-7684-5454-3
ISBN 13 eBook: 978-0-7684-5455-0
ISBN 13 HC: 978-0-7684-5457-4
ISBN 13 LP: 978-0-7684-5456-7

For Worldwide Distribution.

1 2 3 4 5 6 7 8 / 24 23 22 21 20

CONTENTS

Chapter One

A CALL TO THE THRONE ROOM

> *"After this I looked, and, behold, a door was opened in heaven: and the first voice which I heard was as it were of a trumpet talking with me; which said, Come up hither, and I will shew thee things which must be hereafter."*
> —REVELATION 4:1

On the night I was filled with the Holy Spirit in 1984, I had a spiritual encounter that deeply impacted my walk with the Lord and changed me forever. This encounter began my journey into knowing and communicating the heart of the One who is seated on the Throne. In the pages that follow, I have done my best to present some of the key revelations and insights I've gained as a child of God and a prophetic voice over the past thirty-five years.

In June of 1984, I had given my life to the Lord in my parents' basement after my high school graduation. I was so on fire for the Lord, and I knew in my heart what I had with my salvation was real. I was so hungry to know God and to be used of Him. I can honestly say that zeal has never left me in over thirty-five years of serving Him. On the night I was gloriously filled with the Holy Spirit, I spoke in other tongues as the Spirit gave me the utterance, and I had a miraculous, heavenly encounter.

I had been asked to come to a church service and, after the service, to be baptized in the Holy Ghost. I had no knowledge of such a thing, nor had I had any teaching about it. I just figured if it was of the Lord, then I wanted it! There was an older woman there who became my spiritual mother in that season, mentoring me in the Scriptures and the things of God three to four times a week for several years. She lived to be a hundred years of age and just got promoted to Heaven a few years ago. When the service ended that night, she and a few others who'd joined her laid their hands upon me and said, "Receive the Holy Spirit." I immediately began to speak in other tongues like a fluent river. It was not just one word but sentences and paragraphs it seemed. I felt lit up on the inside and so very full of His Spirit, with a sense of supernatural power in me. I couldn't stop this unction of praying in this awesome, unknown heavenly language.

I went home and looked in the mirror and my countenance was lit up. I laid down on my bed and continued to let it flow. I can honestly say I prayed in my new heavenly language the whole night, and it was then that the most amazing thing happened. I was caught up to what I believe was a small glimpse of the Throne Room. I immediately was in a room—not my bedroom, but another room. I heard the most beautiful voices singing and the light, oh the glorious light I saw and experienced all around me! The light initially was so bright that it didn't allow me to see, but only to hear and feel such an amazing presence that I'd never felt before.

As this experience continued, I could then see multitudes gathered around me as I was part of a massive crowd, a choir you could say, that was part of this brilliant light. I could see a river that reflected this bright light, but the amazing part was having the feeling of being pulled into something that was drawing me closer to what I believe was the One who sits upon the Throne, God Himself! I could see a figure seated on something big and magnificent, but I could not see the figure's face or what He was sitting on clearly, just His form, because of the brilliant light that caused me to hide my face. I am not sure how long I was there; it really didn't matter as far as natural time was concerned. I awakened from this experience hearing my mom's voice at the top of the stairs yelling my name, and that's when I suddenly realized it was morning. I'd spent the entire night in the presence of the Lord, and I had been changed!

A CALL TO THE THRONE ROOM

I realized that the spiritual experience I had the night I was filled with the Holy Spirit was a call to the Throne Room. It has marked my life ever since with a strong passion to intimately know the Lord and the awesome responsibility of being entrusted with what He reveals to me to share with others. I also believe that this experience is where I received from Him the call to be one of His Throne Room prophetic vessels in the earth. This is important, as no prophetic gifting or office can come by self-calling or choosing; it only comes by His choosing. This kind of Throne Room experience is what happened to the apostle John in Revelation 4: *"Come up hither, and I will shew thee things which must be hereafter"* (Rev. 4:1). John was being called to the Throne Room. This same call is upon us, especially those who stand in the land to be His Throne Room prophets. In fact, three powerful words that John heard are still being echoed today: "Come up here!" This is an invitation by the Lord to be taken in the Spirit into the presence of God so He can deepen our relationship with Him and also show us prophetic things that must come hereafter.

Like John, though not as dramatic, in my spiritual experience I was being called to "Come up here!" I have come to realize how important that experience was and is, as a call to come up higher and to know the One seated on the Throne. I must know Him so He can entrust me with things He wants to say or reveal. In addition, it was also to teach me how to receive those precious words from the Lord and to hear His secrets. This comes by establishing a consistent relationship that must go beyond what we can receive of Him, through a longing to know who He is. In turn, He then entrusts us with His heart— the most sacred part of who He is. His heart contains His feelings, His thoughts, His likes and dislikes, His intents, and His agenda, to name a few aspects. These wonderful things of His heart are entrusted to us and have been given to us so we can communicate and demonstrate them to others. How is this done? It happens through the gift of prophecy, the office of the prophet, as well as through other ministry gifts and functions. This is why answering the call to come up higher to the Throne Room must be treated with a reverent fear, honor, and respect of not only the place we are being summoned to but, most importantly, the Holy One Himself—the Lord.

It is not hard to discern those who carry the heart of God because they are in a constant state of fellowship with Him and only want to do things that please Him. They model His heart, His character, and His ways. You can sense they have been with God, and what they minister carries the presence of having been in the Throne Room. Their words are filled with power, their character reflects Him, they have His moral standards, and they are jealous with what makes Him jealous. As they speak for Him and minister for Him, it will be said of them as it was of the disciples, that these men have spent time with the Lord. It is from this call to the Throne Room that true Throne Room prophets and prophecy are born and maintained. It is not a one-time pursuit but a lifestyle where everything they desire to speak, to minister, and to reveal has been a result of this call to the Throne Room with Him.

This call to come up higher to the Throne Room is to summon God's people—sons, daughters, men, women, young, and old—to go another level in hearing and speaking for the Lord. This can only be done if we choose to respond to Him. It is especially necessary that we answer the call to the Throne Room so we can effectively discern what are right words, wrong words, wishful words, and false words.

When one spends quality time with God, it is not hard to discern if they are speaking from Heaven or not. Those who have been in the Throne Room speak words that carry the sound and weight of Heaven. It cannot be stressed enough that the call to the Throne Room is a about spending time with God and learning His ways. Our desire must be to know the One who sits on the Throne. Intimacy and relationship must be first and foremost if we are to be entrusted with the sacred heart and words of the Lord. Where Throne Room prophets and prophecy fall short is when the focus is on the prophetic words given rather than on Him. This is why there is a lack of accuracy and even character among those who say they have heard from the Lord. A life committed to knowing Him and spending time with Him in the Throne Room is imperative, especially if we want to be effective ministers for Him.

Knowing the importance of this heavenly place and passionately pursuing God is ultimately the emphasis of John's call to come up higher. We see this in Revelation 4 simply by how many times the Throne of God and the One seated on that Throne are mentioned. It not only shows the importance of the Throne of God but, most importantly, Him who is seated on that Throne. All ministry, especially prophecy, must follow this, not precede it.

COME UP HIGHER

There is a call to come up higher in true Throne Room prophecy. It is as if Heaven is asking, "Who will answer the call to the Throne Room? Who will answer the call to come up higher, to be shown things the Lord wants to tell us to come hereafter?"

If one chooses to answer like John did, it will require us to raise a higher standard in our lives and in the prophetic words we receive and share. In addition, it will require from us a deeper, consistent pursuit and a passionate desire to know Him greater and to be used of Him at a higher level. How do we do this? We need to once again consider the apostle John. He had already been in the Spirit since Revelation 1—the beginning of his encounter with Jesus. This example is the same for anyone who is called as a Throne Room prophet, as well as for all who desire to deliver Throne Room prophecy. We can see that the Lord wanted John to come up even higher, meaning there are deeper levels and standards that we are being summoned to. We must also keep in mind that John was being called to a higher place as a result of decisions he made while he walked with the Lord on earth. Leaning his head upon Jesus' breast was the foundation that preceded him now being called higher.

That same call is going out from the Throne Room in this day, and it is being offered to those who, like John, want the heart of the Lord first and foremost in their daily walk. In this call, God wants the standard, the precision, the revelation, and the demonstration of what we receive from Him to come to another level so that the world will know we are speaking and representing Him.

We must not lower the bar of His call by careless prophetic delivery or undisciplined prophets or prophetic ministers. We cannot afford bad pulpit manners or bad manners in general, prophesying words that are wrong, wishful, false, or flakey. A call to come up higher is a call to raise our expectations, our discipline, and our desire to have a sure word of prophecy in our mouths and lives. It is a call to speak words that are filled with the Spirit of Truth, that would never ever want to bring reproach to Him or the gift and giftings He has given us.

God summoned John higher so He could show him things that were to come at a higher level and so John could accurately share them. God's heart or pulse requires a voice, a spokesman to release it in the earth. Remember, the Lord does nothing in the earth without revealing it to His servants, the prophets (see Amos 3:7).

A call to a higher level and a deeper dimension with Him is what He wants from us. It is what the Lord intended for John, and it's what He desires for His prophets today. As I mentioned, John was already in the Spirit on the Lord's day, but this was another level of spiritual revelation, manifestation, and experience. John had already had a definitive experience of walking with Jesus on the earth, representing our walk with the Lord in this natural realm. It was thereafter that his experiences deepened with this visitation and manifestation of Jesus in the power of His resurrection, which opened his spiritual eyes to see and experience Him on another level. This, again, was a higher place, dimension, and manifestation of a spiritual experience that comes through the Holy Spirit and His power. It was an even higher summoning to reveal greater dimensions and levels. It was a call to the Throne Room to see Jesus not just as the earthly Christ he'd experienced or the resurrected Christ, but the Ascended Christ in all His glory! It was from this place in the Throne Room that a higher level of responsibility, revelation, and spiritual manifestation took place.

This is where the Throne Room prophets must spend most of their time. It is not so much just ministering and experiencing the Lord on earth or the manifestations of the anointing; it's not so much the Spirit of resurrection power, though all these things are absolutely vital. This call is to come up higher to a Throne Room life of encounters with Him and should be the passionate desire of every believer and prophetic vessel. It is what gives you heavenly accuracy, power, and backing from the Lord God Himself, making your ministry more effective in the earth. Through this Throne Room life, you can avoid the need to appear "super-spiritual," and you won't be prophetically flakey or act immature in your gifting and function.

An example of Heaven's backing and authority on a life well-grounded in a deep relationship with the Father is when Jesus sat down to speak, teach, and minister. Scripture uses a Greek word *kathizo* for many of those times when He sat down (Strong's, G2523). This word is used over fifty times in the New Testament and is often used when speaking of seats of authority and power like judicial, governmental, and religious power. This means that when Jesus sat down, though He was on earth, He was speaking and ministering from the place of the Throne Room with authority and power, backed by the Father, because He spent daily quality time with Him. We can clearly see this as Jesus sat in various places, like on a rock and in the boat, for example. It was not the only place of authority that He was speaking from or representing, but rather, He was speaking from a position of heavenly authority and backing at the same time! This is the meaning and understanding of this word, *kathizo,* and is the prototype of what it means to come up higher. It is what God wants His vessels in the earth to always remember as they are seated with Him or standing to minister for Him. It is who they're representing or speaking for, and their words must come from the Throne Room with demonstrated authority and power, like Jesus' words! Remember, Jesus was able to speak from this higher place of authority and accuracy because of the time He spent with the Father. He was consistently found in prayer—morning, noon, and night. He answered the call to come up higher, the call to the Throne Room, and so must we!

Again, it is important to remember that the call to come up higher is to take us to another level with Him and with things He chooses to entrust us with.

We can see that the Lord has no problem bringing us to a greater level of His glory, as we see in Ezekiel 47. Here we find four different levels of the glory of God and the flow of His power. This was the experience that Ezekiel, a Throne Room prophet, had when he stepped into the river of God. He found that the depth was ankle, knee, waist deep, and that which he could swim in. The deeper he was taken in this river of glory, the more skill and understanding of the depth would be required. For example, he could splash in ankle-deep water without much skill or understanding. However, to enter the deep water where he could only swim would require more skill, technique, and understanding due to the level of the water.

It is the same way when it comes to Throne Room prophecy and going deeper with the Lord and the spiritual words and encounters. It will require less flesh and a more focused understanding of the depth you are being taken into. Mature prophets and prophetic people who experience the deep are recognized not so much by the deep revelations and experiences that they share, but rather, by the things they don't share. In other words, they are disciplined, trained by the Lord, and they don't have to prove anything because they have been changed by Him and are yielded to Him. They aren't sloppy with the prophetic, always having to pull someone aside with a word or push to be seen and heard. The character and the maturity of gifting is revealed in their discipline of holding on to the word of the Lord and knowing when, how, if, and with whom to share their experiences. They are content in not being the focus of attention or being measured as a deep prophet or prophetic minister by the level of their revelations or experiences.

When Peter, James, and John were being taken to a higher level or depth in the things of the Lord, they were overcome with the fear of the Lord.

> *While he yet spake, behold, a bright cloud overshadowed them: and behold a voice out of the cloud, which said, This is my beloved Son, in whom I am well pleased; hear ye him. And when the disciples heard it, they fell on their face, and were sore afraid* (Matthew 17:5-6).

They were also instructed by Jesus not to share their experience of seeing the Lord transfigured in glory.

And as they came down from the mountain, Jesus charged them, saying, Tell the vision to no man, until the Son of man be risen again from the dead (Matthew 17:9).

Being in His presence, like they were at Jesus' transfiguration and when John was in the Spirit in the Throne Room, will change you, making you more effective in hearing and delivering Throne Room prophecy. His powerful presence is the result of answering this call to come up higher and will reveal areas where we are undone and even areas that we need to improve.

Think about this for a moment: Isaiah was a Throne Room prophet who got a glimpse of the Throne Room. He said in the midst of his experience, *"Then said I, Woe is me! for I am undone; because I am a man of unclean lips"* (Isa. 6:5). He says this because he is in the presence of God Himself, and this will always bring proper perspective of who He is, who we are, and what we need to become. Spending time in God's presence is what marks a true Throne Room prophet and Throne Room prophecy. They have allowed the Lord to make them, mold them, change them, and use them. It is evident not so much in their prophecies or revelation but in the fruit of their ministry, revealed in character and the manifestation of their giftings. We can learn a valuable lesson from Isaiah about the importance of allowing God to change and shape us. Isaiah realized his human frailty needed the help of God in order to correctly speak for the Lord and minister as His representative.

Speaking the Lord's words comes with a price, especially when called to stand as a Throne Room prophet. Not everyone who prophesies is a prophet as described in Ephesians 4:11. This verse tells us Jesus gave *some* to be prophets, not all. Yet if you are called to be a Throne Room prophet, you must allow the Lord to make and take you through the process of becoming His mouthpiece and spokesman. The office of the prophet should never be taken lightly as it is one of the most misunderstood and persecuted offices and giftings the Lord has given. I know firsthand the price, the journey, the ups and downs, the misunderstandings, the persecutions, and the awesome fear of being entrusted with His heart and words. As you see with the prophets of Scripture, they didn't have an easy journey in their molding and making to become God's prophetic vessels.

When I hear people identify themselves as prophets, I often take a moment and wonder if they really know the journey, the price of what they identify with. It is no joke, no status symbol, or anything to treat lightly. It should come with a holy fear, awe, and strong desire to have a sure word of prophecy in our mouths that is coupled with the Spirit of Truth. We should rather say nothing than to be wrong or misrepresent the Lord and what He is revealing. Yet, at the same time, you are faithful to open your mouth when He speaks and tells you, and you do it with honor and obedience to Him as a servant unto the people to whom He sends you.

Like with Isaiah who saw the Lord high and lifted up in Isaiah 6:1, this needs to be our focus—to see the Lord high and lifted up, not ourselves. We must realize that the things we are being entrusted to receive, whether seen, heard, or perceived, are to glorify Him who sits on the Throne. The testimony of Jesus is the Spirit of prophecy, meaning that glorifying God and testifying of Him is the real motive behind the Throne Room prophet. It isn't about taking the credit for healings, fulfilled prophecies, or any other wonderful thing the Lord does.

A Throne Room prophet is unique in character and gifting because they exemplify the heart of God and what He has given them to share with others. It is those who never allow Him to mold them, humble them, and bring them through the often-lonely journey required to represent Him who wind up not lasting long in ministry. This refusal to be shaped by God also often leads to self-promotion, immaturity, an unteachable spirit, lack of accountability, and pride. If these things take center stage, they become the focal points rather than the Lord, and we cannot accurately reflect Him in gifting and character. Note that Isaiah's call to the Throne Room and this higher spiritual dimension brought out his weakness and vulnerability and created a deep fear of the Lord as he said, *"Woe is me! for I am undone."*

The apostle Paul is another example of what happens when we are summoned higher to the Throne Room. When he was caught up to the third heaven, it revealed areas in him that required growth. Notice how he speaks about his weakness and his desire, not wanting to be prideful or draw attention to himself, his message, or his experience. He was even reluctant to tell anyone his visions or revelations. This is always a must for those who want to be trusted with a higher level of Throne Room prophecy. Not every experience is meant to be shared, and out of respect to the Lord we must wait for His leading. A great self-test is not to be too quick to share every vision, dream, and prophecy to every person or audience. Ask yourself, "Does the Lord want me to speak this? How is this going to affect those with whom I share it? What is my motive in sharing what I receive?" In doing so, you will fine-tune your ear and skill to operate at an even higher level of prophetic things. It is an example for us who desire to go to another level as a Throne Room prophet or one who ministers Throne Room prophecy.

It is important that we are yielded to the Lord in areas where we need adjustment and growth. As we can see with Paul, his weakness was brought out to change him, grow him, and keep him in the right spirit during his time in the Throne Room.

> *This boasting will do no good, but I must go on. I will reluctantly tell about visions and revelations from the Lord. I was caught up to the third heaven fourteen years ago. Whether I was in my body or out of my body, I don't know—only God knows. Yes, only God knows whether I was in my body or outside my body. But I do know that I was caught up to paradise and heard things so astounding that they cannot be expressed in words, things no human is allowed to tell. That experience is worth boasting about, but I'm not going to do it. I will boast only about my weaknesses. If I wanted to boast, I would be no fool in doing so, because I would be telling the truth. But I won't do it, because I don't want*

anyone to give me credit beyond what they can see in my life or hear in my message, even though I have received such wonderful revelations from God. So to keep me from becoming proud... (2 Corinthians 12:1-7 NLT).

When one allows God to take them through the necessary process and preparation to be His prophet or a believer who prophesies, it should not be hard to discern those who are true Throne Room prophets or if a prophecy is from the Lord. It becomes easier to discern both what we receive from the Lord and those who deliver a prophetic word. How do we know? We can discern by their fruit, by whether their time with God reflects in their character and not just in their gifting. When a person is changed by the Throne Room, instead of pride, conceit, selfish ambition, or a need to be the center of attention, they display qualities like vulnerability, humility, and especially a strong fear of the Lord with a strong reliance upon Him. This will help you to discern the ones ministering as well as the prophetic words given. Those who spend genuine time with God will manifest the fruit and character of having been with Him. Their agenda will not be to impress man or have the most followers on their social media platforms but to glorify, honor, and minister with the fear of the Lord in their hearts. As they stand in awe of Him, the fear of the Lord spills over onto the ones they're ministering to.

I believe we can often tell if a person is spending quality time in the Throne Room by first, the focus: is it the Lord or ourselves? Second, what is more important, my gifting, anointing, or how God uses me; or is it ministering effectively to others, making them the priority? Third, what kind of character do we display, as well as the power manifested? As we saw with the apostle Paul's Throne Room experience, the Lord is willing to reach out in response to us, but something else also takes place as we spend time in His presence. His presence will humble you, focus you, make you, break you, and mold you. It will give you experiences that you can share with others, encouraging them to answer His consistent call to come up higher into the Throne Room. Spend time with Him and He will share His secrets with you! *"Ask me and I will tell you remarkable secrets you do not know about things to come"* (Jer. 33:3 NLT).

Their time with the One who is seated upon the Throne as the Lord of all is what sets apart prophets and those who prophesy in the earth. They are changed, trained, and developed in His presence. This is not a one-time glorious experience but a habit that should span our whole lifetime of serving the Lord. It also will be what causes others to trust that the words we are prophesying are truly coming from the Lord.

REACH OUT AND HE WILL REACH BACK

In the call to come up higher it is vital that we understand the importance of knowing Him first and foremost, rather than just seeking Him for what He will reveal to us. When we remember this, He begins to speak and reveal much to us, particularly to Throne Room prophets, because that is their entrusted spiritual assignment and positional authority. I have personally learned what happens when you answer the call to come up higher and make your life, ministry, and gifting all about the pursuit of Him and what He wants. He then reaches back, building an amazing relationship of discussion, secrets between just you and Him, and many spiritual experiences—some to be shared and others to be secretly treasured. The greater our experience is with Him, the greater things He will reveal and manifest to others through us. He is the center of attention, the One receiving the glory.

Once you establish this foundation, then go ahead in your relationship by asking Him, "What's on Your heart, Lord? What would You like to say, reveal, and manifest to bless others?" Make it about Him first and then, second, ministering to others. When you do, He will reach back to you and through you in a greater way!

I remember when the Lord called my wife Brenda and I to serve Him on Christian television nationally and internationally. This was a big step for us as we weren't seeking to be on television and really hadn't done so before. I was in my basement praying over partners and those who had written in prayer requests. We scattered these requests across our house on the floor and we would pray over them and be reminded how important their requests were and why the Lord was calling us to utilize the tool of television. I was holding a large pile of them in my arms when I felt something shift in the room by way of the Lord's presence. It was then that I turned and looked to the other side of the basement to someone I know was Jesus standing there looking at me. I really believe to this day I saw Him and that He literally opened my eyes to see Him standing there. What really touched me was as I held these requests, the tighter I held them the more He reached out His arms. I then heard these words in my heart: "Hank, always remember this call to television for you and Brenda is first about Me as your focus and then it is about the people and their needs." I knew how true this was, and the tighter I held those prayer requests to my chest (my heart), the more He opened His arms. It was a great lesson to me to always remember that all true ministry and power to meet people's needs comes from Him. It must not be about us, but Him and His desire to reach others through us.

Through that experience, the Lord was showing me that when we reach out to Him, He will reach back to us, through us, and for us. We must answer the call to the Throne Room and be willing to come up higher. When we do, we receive not only what we need but also are positioned to deliver His answers to others.

This actually happened in a powerful experience I had recently. I was awakened to the sound of the most beautiful male singing voice that I have ever heard in my life. I have never felt the peace, the comfort, the strength, or the presence I felt that day. As I opened my eyes, once again I saw that bright light that I'd seen when I was filled with the Holy Spirit. Again, it filled my eyes so that I couldn't see, but I could hear. I heard this voice say, "This was Me singing to you, Hank!"

I said, "Lord, that was You?"

He replied, "Yes, as My Word declares that I rejoice over you with singing!" I was in utter shock that I was literally sung to by the Lord Himself. This is what I mean when I say that when we reach out and determine to come up higher, to love Him more, spend time with Him more, hunger for more of Him and with passion to serve Him, He reaches back.

If that wasn't enough, a week later I was awakened again to a sound of glorious singing and music. It filled my bedroom, my whole being, and it was so, so glorious. I began to sing along with what seemed to be a heavenly choir and we were all singing the same words. We were as one singing, "How great is our God!" When I awoke, I was still singing those words with all my inner being. Strangely, no sound came out of my mouth, just the sound of a quiet whisper—even though it seemed like I was singing at the top of my lungs. It was a good thing that it happened that way, as it might have woken my wife, Brenda, who was still sleeping next to me! My point in sharing this encounter is, reach out and He *will* reach back. Learn to listen to those urges and sudden desires that come to you throughout the day to come away to worship, pray, listen, and fellowship with Him in the Throne Room. When you do so, you have answered the call to come up higher where He can show you things like He showed the apostle John, things that will come hereafter.

You might be saying, "That will never happen to me." Why not? This is available to any child of God, but it's specifically necessary for those called as Throne Room prophets. It must be noted that to come up higher will require, time, pursuit, and consistency. It is a lifelong commitment and not to be thought of as an occasional visit. Our spiritual maturity, senses, and hearing are greatly developed when we prioritize a life before

His Throne. This is what will take us from being a lamb in our innocence and immaturity to a mature sheep in character, anointing, and our ability to hear from Him. Jesus even said, *"My sheep hear my voice"* (John 10:27). Notice it is a process of going from a young lamb to a mature sheep.

It is this desire to grow and mature, regardless of how long we have been serving the Lord, that will help us not only return to but also strive for words from the Lord that carry the anointing and utterance of His Spirit. It has been prophesied that these days we are living in will be marked with an increase of the prophetic. This includes the young and old prophesying and having visions and dreams.

> *In the last days, God says, I will pour out my Spirit on all people. Your sons and daughters will prophesy, your young men will see visions, your old men will dream dreams. Even on my servants, both men and women, I will pour out my Spirit in those days, and they will prophesy* (Acts 2:17-18 NIV).

We can see from this verse that it was as a result of the Holy Spirit being poured out that manifestations of prophecy, visions, and dreams would come about. Always remember that it is the Holy Spirit who will bring the manifestation of these things and it is by the Spirit that we operate at a higher level. It is important to know this because we don't want prophecy that is not from the Holy Spirit. When we seek to prophesy at a higher level without the Holy Spirit's leading, the result will be soulish or fleshly "prophecy" that is not given by Him. It will be prophecy that is driven by our own soul, meaning it will come from our mind, will, and emotions. In fact, it is this type of "prophecy" that defines not necessarily false prophecy, but wrong prophecy, which we will discuss in a later chapter. It is not necessarily false, meaning it is not purposely seeking to deceive or it doesn't carry a false spirit with it. Instead, it is wrong and without a purposeful meaning, coming from the mind and emotions of the person speaking. This makes it a wrong prophecy.

We need the Holy Spirit, as He is and should be the "Spirit" of prophecy in which we learn to flow. The apostles knew the importance of always placing the Holy Spirit first. It is recorded in Acts 15:28 that *"it seemed good to the Holy Ghost, and to us."* They understood it must be good unto God *first*, not last or not at all. We should never try to minister on our own without the Holy Ghost involved. Sadly, this type of thing goes on in some prophetic circles more often than we want to admit. There are those who seem to love prophecy more than they love the God of the prophetic. No matter what, they want to hear a word! This kind of mindset drives many people to prophesy in the flesh out of an effort to fulfil this demand for a "word" to be spoken. My concern is, does God still have a say in whether we share a word or keep silent, whether we minister or not?

The more we are including Him and open to Him, the more we will increase in our accuracy and in the levels that we prophesy. When we remember the importance of ministering with the Holy Spirit, it will help us go higher in our anointings and giftings. This is because we are being guided by the Spirit—when He says speak, we speak; but if He instructs us to be silent, we are disciplined to do so. It is critical that we don't speak just because someone wants us to. In addition, keeping the Holy Spirit in the forefront will also help us to truly discern those who are standing in the place of Throne Room prophetic. When we do this, our spirit will bear witness with His Spirit when something is being prophesied. We literally feel and recognize when the Holy Spirit is upon it!

It is so necessary for the times in which we live, when so many voices and opinions are expressed, that we make a determined effort to work with the Holy Spirit. It will help keep us from prophesying out of our own souls instead of by His Spirit. This is especially true when prophecies are dealing with very specific and directional words, rather than prophetic words that offer a simple word of exhortation, edification, or comfort.

Now more than ever, we must have Holy Spirit-bred and led prophets and prophetic people. Scripture tells us that people are going to turn to the words of the prophets in these times. *"Disaster will come upon disaster and rumor will be added to rumor; then they will seek a vision from a prophet"* (Ezek. 7:26 NASB). You can see from this verse the important role prophets have in bringing clarity in troubling times and truth when rumors dominate what people believe. They help us to correctly understand what is happening in the spiritual realm and in the earth. This is because any true understanding of the course of world events must be based on Heaven's perspective of those events. It requires that we see and understand with our spiritual senses, especially our spiritual eyes, which give us the proper perspective in not only discerning a prophecy but also giving a prophetic word.

"I WILL SHOW YOU THINGS THAT MUST BE HEREAFTER"

It is so important that we have the right perspective, seeing correctly with our spiritual eyes and discerning accurately with our spiritual ears. When John heard the first voice that spoke to him, saying, *"Come up hither, and I will shew thee things which must be hereafter"* (Rev. 4:1), he responded to two things. First, John received the call to come up higher; and second, he responded to the declaration that he'd see things that would happen in the future. Both the call and the declaration were from the Throne Room perspective, and the source of that perspective was God Himself. Our Throne Room prophecies must carry Heaven's perspective and come from the very heart of God, which is the true perspective we seek.

In receiving these heavenly perspectives, it is interesting to note one of the things that caught John's attention. It was the four faces of four beasts that he saw—a lion, an ox, a man, and an eagle. We will discuss these in detail in Chapter Seven, but for now let's look at one of the instances where John mentions seeing eyes in the Throne Room. He saw, for example, these four faces, having eyes within and without.

> *Each of these living beings had six wings, and their wings were covered all over with eyes, inside and out* (Revelation 4:8 NLT).

What does this represent? These eyes prophetically speak of our perspective and perceptions, both spiritually and naturally speaking. Having eyes inside represents our spiritual eyes and our prophetic senses within us, which aid us in attaining a Throne Room level of prophecy. Our eyes without represent our natural eyes and perception. We need both as they help us to correctly discern the word of the Lord and what the Lord is doing, both in Heaven and on earth.

It is crucial that we don't misread what is happening in the spirit and the earth at this time, and this is why a genuine level of Throne Room prophecy is so needed right now. We must have the right prophetic perspective, or we won't have the correct interpretation of things that are happening in the earth. For example, we see Jesus in Mark 6 sending His disciples to go ahead of Him in the boat as He would stay behind and pray. It is interesting to note the importance of perspective. We find in this story that the Lord was able to correctly discern in the Spirit what was happening with the disciples when they were in the middle of the sea caught in a storm. The Scripture says in Mark 6:48 that Jesus saw the disciples were having a hard time in the middle of the sea due to the wind that was contrary to them. How would Jesus have known this? He wouldn't have been able to see three to four miles out into the sea in the midst of the storm, as the Bible records. It was due to His connection to the One seated on the Throne, His Father. He received this information by spiritual perception that caused Him to have the right perspective regarding what was happening to the disciples.

The story continues and we again see the importance of the right perspective as Jesus was walking on the sea toward the disciples and they were very afraid. So afraid, in fact, that they had the wrong perspective, thinking they were seeing a ghost rather than Jesus! In the same way today, when prophetic ministers yield themselves or are influenced by a contrary spirit like fear, they will always prophesy an inaccurate word or perspective. This is what happened with the disciples. Their perspective was based on what they were personally experiencing, coupled with a spirit of fear. It caused them to not discern what was happening correctly, both in the spirit and the natural, as Jesus was walking on the water.

This often is why we hear doom and gloom prophecies that in the end never produce what was prophesied. It's because those prophesying either were basing their words on their own experiences or they were yielding to a contrary spirit or contrary "wind," like the disciples did, rather than yielding to the Spirit of God. It causes them to not have the right perspective of what is happening, and as a result their words carry the very spirit that they are ministering from—a spirit of fear.

It is only as we determine to allow God to take us higher that revelation at a higher level will be given, giving us His perspective and His agenda and making our words and ministry more accurate. Remember, this is what happened to the apostle John. He had to answer the call to come up higher; only then would he get to see and know what would come next, giving him a proper prophetic perspective.

We must never get that backwards, as immature or untaught prophetic vessels often do. Some desire to be shown heavenly things, but they are preoccupied with wanting to be seen as having a great prophetic gift. Others mistakenly think that they are the only ones with revelation on a particular matter. However, when this is their posture, these vessels haven't yet paid a price to go higher in the Throne Room encounter. They haven't truly been changed by Him, and it is reflected in their character, words, and ministry. This often can be seen by the inaccurate perspectives revealed in their teachings or prophecies. What do I mean? When you have the Throne Room encounter, you have the Throne Room perspective. The Throne Room perspective isn't based on the words of the land, meaning the perspective of everything around you that comes through the media or others. You don't have to scroll the internet for the latest prophetic words and make them your own; instead, you have personally received from the Lord because you have been with Him and He has spoken to you. In fact, this practice of taking other prophets' words and making them yours did not go well with the Lord and was often the mark of a false prophet. *"Therefore, behold, I am against the prophets, saith the Lord, that steal my words every one from his neighbour"* (Jer. 23:30). Today, this will lead someone down a path to eventually becoming wrong or false in their prophecies because they rely on what others say when they have not heard for themselves.

This is why it is so necessary that we get the right perspective for ourselves. I am not implying or saying we can't be inspired by other prophetic words or vessels or receive inspiration that unlocks something in us, including the voice of the Lord. What I am saying is this: if we take other people's prophecies or prophetic words without hearing for ourselves and put our "thus saith the Lord" on them, then it becomes other people's perspectives that we are taking credit for. It was not what we received from God during our own times with Him. Those who make a practice of this can eventually not only misrepresent the Lord but themselves. In addition, it will cause the gifting we've been given, or Heaven's perspective that has been entrusted to us, to result in confusion. It can ultimately cause people to despise and mistrust the prophetic. We must each allow the Lord to adjust us and personally give us a correct perspective and revelation, so that those listening can receive and rejoice at the words we share. We can't just get that from someone else.

Attaining this right heavenly perspective means we need to answer a simple question that Jesus asked a blind man who was being changed by His presence. The question the Lord asked is found in Mark 8:23: *"What do you see?"* This is also the question the Lord is asking those who desire to minister in Throne Room prophecy. Now, let's consider this story further. This man was blind from birth and wanted to be healed, so Jesus took him out of the city. Why out of the city? It is because man built the city. As long as the man was in the city, he would see what man built. So Jesus took him out of the city to an open place where God had made the hills, the grass, and the trees. When the man would open his eyes, he would see not man's perspective but God's. He would see what God created—God's perspective. This man was gloriously healed and saw men walking as trees. Jesus then prayed for this man a second time to fully receive his sight. I believe this offers us a prophetic meaning. It reveals that having our perspective adjusted to Heaven's is not just a one-time thing. It is a process that should span our whole lives and spiritual journey.

There are times we are going to need Jesus to "open our eyes" a second time!

This truth is underscored in First Corinthians 13:9, which says we know in part and prophesy in part. We have to remember that we don't know everything and we should never act as though we do! We need to be cautious of those who always have a prophetic answer for everything.

We are always growing and increasing in our revelation knowledge. The Lord wants to continually increase our spiritual perception and even the level we are operating at currently. It is why there was a particular anointing on Jesus when He announced His ministry in Luke 4; He declared He was anointed to bring a *"recovery of sight to the blind."* We sometimes see this as Jesus coming to open the eyes of lost sinners, but it's also something the Lord will continually do for us throughout our walk with Him. Areas of spiritual blindness are being continually healed in our lives, enabling us to see more clearly.

Another way we increase our spiritual perception and perspective is to remind ourselves of what Jesus said regarding our lives in the earth. He said, *"men's hearts failing them for fear and for looking after those things which are coming on the earth: for the powers of heaven shall be shaken"* (Luke 21:26).

This is because what you see going on around you can and will sometimes formulate or even dominate your spiritual perception and perspective. Instead of spending time listening to the report of the news or the land, look up and learn to come higher to receive Heaven's perspective. I have learned that what often marks a Throne Room prophet and those who prophesy

Throne Room words is that what they share is usually contrary to the popular trends, discussions, and proverbs that are being resounded in the earth.

We must always remember that prophets in the Bible were often stoned unjustly because it sometimes appeared as if their words did not, or were not, coming to pass. Think about the prophetic words of John, Isaiah, Jeremiah, and even Ezekiel, to name a few. Many of the words they gave are still in the process of coming to pass. The bottom line is, one of the most challenging things for any prophet is the timing of the prophetic revelation they're being shown from the Lord, like John who saw things coming in the present or future. This is why it is wise not to judge a prophetic word too quickly, deeming it as false or wrong when it might be a true word from the Lord. Perhaps it just needs time to breathe, meaning it needs time for the manifestation to happen.

Now, if a specific time was mentioned in a prophetic word and it didn't happen in that time frame, it may be that the hearer put their own timing or expectation on it. Or it might be a right word given but wrong timing. We also need to consider that it might have been a right word and even right timing, but the timing was delayed by human choices or the enemy's interference. This is due to prophecy being conditional as Paul instructed the Corinth church—that we *"know in part, and we prophesy in part"* (1 Cor. 13:9). We don't know everything, including timing.

Think about the word God gave to and through Moses to Israel of a promised land flowing with milk and honey. It was not meant to be a forty-year journey but only a few days. It didn't make the prophecy, or even Moses himself, false or wrong. The word became conditional based upon the decisions of the children of Israel. Their poor choices prolonged their journey and delayed the word of the Lord to them.

This is the challenge of knowing and seeing in part or partially. Not any one of us knows everything. In fact, the Bible says we see through a glass darkly (see 1 Cor. 13:12). Let's again consider what we mentioned about prophecy being conditional. The New Living Translation says it very well in First Corinthians 13:9, which says, *"Now our knowledge is partial and incomplete, and even the gift of prophecy reveals only part of the whole picture!"* This is why prophets came from the high places together.

> *After that thou shalt come to the hill of God, where is the garrison of the Philistines: and it shall come to pass, when thou art come thither to the city, that thou shalt meet a company of prophets coming down from the high place with a psaltery, and a tabret, and a pipe, and a harp, before them; and they shall prophesy* (1 Samuel 10:5).

It was each prophet hearing and receiving from the Lord who added their individual parts of revelation that helped them understand what God was saying collectively. This is why we must never assume we have the whole picture of what God is doing. It takes many of us adding our parts together so the world gains the whole perspective!

We need to stand with those who are receiving the Lord's perspective from the place of the Throne Room. They have the ability to discern through the fearful events and darkness around us and give God's perspective because they have been with Him.

So how do we come up higher and receive a deeper understanding and heavenly perspective that aids us in the prophetic? It is found in the three ways that the apostle John was able to receive Throne Room or Heaven's perspective and is the same for us who desire Throne Room prophecy.

> *After this I looked, and, behold, a door was opened in heaven: and the first voice which I heard was as it were of a trumpet talking with me; which said, Come up hither, and I will shew thee things which must be hereafter. And immediately I was in the spirit* (Revelation 4:1-2).

These are the primary ways God communicates His perspective to us: first, it comes by something we see—John looked and saw. Second, it may come by something we hear as with John, who heard a noise. Third, it can be through something we perceive or feel, like the way John knew he was in the Spirit. In the same way, when we are learning to receive or position ourselves to be entrusted with Throne Room prophecy and receive Heaven's perspective, we will usually see, hear, feel, or perceive what the Lord is communicating.

I want to encourage you to make it your strong daily discipline to walk with the Lord and spend time with Him. Desire for Him to take you higher in the things of His Spirit, to get a true glimpse of who He really is as the One seated on the Throne. Ask Him to take you higher in Him and in what He chooses to show you. Then be ready, because He will begin to show you more in-depth things that will not only bless you and others, but He will set you on a journey to be a vessel of honor with true Throne Room prophecy in your mouth!

Chapter Two

THE HEART OF THE THRONE ROOM

"And immediately I was in the spirit: and, behold, a throne was set in heaven, and one sat on the throne."
—REVELATION 4:2

I've been collecting model trains for most of my life and building my HO-scale layout for over a decade. It is my favorite hobby and I often enjoy time with the Lord as I'm working on my trains. There was one day, though, where the Lord caught me by surprise and I experienced a tremendous heavenly vision.

I was working on my trains, sitting at my hobby desk and thinking of the Sunday service the following day, which happened to be Resurrection Sunday. I was going over my message in my head and praying in the Spirit while I built a structure for the train layout. At one point, I decided to take a break

from my project and knelt next to my chair to worship the Lord. As I sang to Him with my eyes closed, I suddenly felt prompted to open my eyes, only to have a heavenly vision as real as the very chair in front of me and the floor below me. Two feet wearing sandals appeared standing before me as I was kneeling there. I was so overwhelmed by what I was seeing and experiencing; I remember crying and trying to get as low to the ground as I could to show my honor to the Lord. I knew these were His feet appearing before me. I was so overcome by His love; the fear of the Lord gripped my heart, but at the same time I had such a sense of being accepted by Him. He was the focus; nothing else mattered to me—not me, not my trains, not anything else.

From the moment of the Lord's feet appearing before me, He was the total focus. I could see nothing else. Though I had a vastly different experience, He showed me that day what He'd shown the apostle John—that He is always to be the focus and center of our attention.

Nothing else matters or deserves our full attention except Him. No ministry can be effective—not one minister, prophet, or any person with any gifting—unless the Lord is center stage. Keeping the Lord as our focus will keep us grounded and centered on Him and will help us discern genuine prophecy and the prophetic. It will also aid us in keeping the right spirit when discerning prophecy and those who prophesy, because we will not make false judgments and critiques. The reason this happens is because the more we spend time with the Lord, the more we become like Him, recognizing what is from Him and what resembles Him.

To give a natural example, in any room I can recognize and single out my wife's voice as being hers because I have spent over three decades married to her. In the same way, the more we spend time with God, the more we recognize His voice and the way He communicates to us. The more familiar we are with His voice, the more we will be able to discern His voice when it is being spoken through others. We will be better able to discern whether the one speaking is speaking for the Lord or if they are speaking from their own spirit, or perhaps even from an evil spirit. When we are familiar with His voice, we are sharpened in our discernment and able to recognize the source of the voices that speak to us.

When the apostle John mentions the Throne he saw in Heaven, it's clear that his focus was not on the Throne itself but on the One seated on that Throne.

> *And immediately I was in the spirit: and, behold, a throne was set in heaven, and one sat on the throne* (Revelation 4:2).

The Throne was awesome and glorious to behold. Yet it was not the focal point or the thing that stood out to him the most! It was the *One* who sat on the Throne. This point is so vital to us experiencing a healthy Christian walk with Him, but it's also a key in increasing our spiritual perception, accuracy, and gifting. When the Lord Himself is not the focus or motive, it often can lead to other things becoming the focus or center stage in our lives. This is where those who desire to prophesy can miss it, allowing their focus to become themselves, their ministry, gifting, calling, or even the words they receive from

God. The question we should always ask ourselves to keep us in self-examination without condemnation is, "Do we love Him for who He is, or is it about what we receive from Him and how it makes us look to others when we prophesy?" Prophecy and gifting have their place to be a blessing. However, if we are to mature in Throne Room prophecy, we must make sure that prophecy, ministry, and calling don't become out of balance or overbearing. When they do, the focus becomes on the words given rather than the One who gives prophetic words— the Lord.

Genuine prophecy and our Christian walk must always be about God, His heart, His feelings, and His ways first and foremost! This will bring a spirit of humility upon us and greatly enhance the way we are trusted by the Lord with the things He desires to share. True Throne Room prophets are effective as they come to understand that the priority is not what they are hearing from God but their true intimacy with Him that allows revelation to come forth.

THE ONE SEATED ON THE THRONE

Passion for the *One* seated on the Throne must always be the priority of the Throne Room prophet and anyone who desires to operate deeper in Throne Room prophecy. No matter who we are or what we desire to do for Him, we must be determined to truly come to understand Him and to know Him intimately! This was the cry of the apostle Paul's heart in his writing to the Philippian church:

*That I may know him, and the power of his resurrec-
tion, and the fellowship of his sufferings, being made
conformable unto his death* (Philippians 3:10).

As we can see in this verse, he first mentions his desire
to know God, meaning that he is in pursuit of His heart and
wants to know as much about Him as is humanly possible.
This must be our strong passion as well—so much to the point
that we want to know His character, feelings, secrets, and how
we can be a blessing to Him more than anything else. Notice
how Paul prioritized knowing the Lord first *before* experiencing the power of His resurrection (the power He manifests in
us and through us). This must not be out of order, where we
place wanting to see manifestations of His power ahead of our
pursuit of Him. If this happens, the anointing, prophecy, or
the other ways God is using us can become the focus, and we
can become the center of attention. There is nothing wrong
with emphasizing how God uses us, but we must keep that
in check and make sure our focus is on the Lord. We must
be able to ask ourselves if we have allowed these things to get
us out of balance. A good way to know if we are out of balance is by examining what we spend the most time talking
about. Do we spend a lot of time talking about ourselves and
our accomplishments? Do we need to share our dreams, revelations, visions, and prophecies more than we share about our
relationship with Him? If so, then we are placing power over a
passion for Him!

Remember, Paul spoke of knowing Him *first* and *then* the
power of His resurrection. He also mentions something we

often don't want to include—sharing in the fellowship of His sufferings. What does this mean? This is not talking about our good Father in Heaven giving you a horrible disease or causing a tragedy so you might "suffer with Him." That is not His character, nor does He put something upon you that has been canceled through and by the shed blood of His Son, our Lord Jesus Christ. It means that if we identify with Him as His followers, we will share in suffering with Him through persecution and attacks of the enemy that come simply from being a part of His Body.

> *Remember the word that I said unto you, The servant is not greater than his lord. If they have persecuted me, they will also persecute you* (John 15:20).

As believers, we will also partake in suffering with Him concerning the giftings and callings that He's given us. This is especially true with the prophetic. If you want to operate in true prophecy or you have been chosen by the Lord to be a Throne Room prophet, then you will suffer for the sake of the calling and gifting He's given. In the Bible, prophets sent by the Lord were falsely accused, stoned, and murdered because of the prophetic words they gave. This is what Scripture means when it says the blood of Abel *and* the blood of the prophets still speak today, according to Jesus in Luke 11:51 and Hebrews 12:24. Modern-day prophets are also persecuted or "stoned," you could say, because of the gift they have been given and the prophetic utterances they speak. Prophetic words can be misunderstood or misinterpreted. People often pass judgment based on what they see with their natural eyes. Some folks are malicious and resort to personal attacks. These are, unfortunately, realities of life for those whom God has called to be Throne Room prophets or to be entrusted with Throne Room prophecy. If you are walking in a prophetic gifting or calling, you will have to let criticisms, critiques, and the opinions of others roll off your back. If you're not grounded in an intimate relationship with the Lord, this will affect the effectiveness of your gifting.

Now, this is not to excuse poor behavior on the part of some ministers or prophets. Every person who speaks and prophesies should have accountability and proper ethics in order, and we will address these things in this book. The point is that if you are going to speak for the Lord prophetically, you must also be willing to share in His suffering and pay the price to be part of His Body and called of Him.

The apostle Paul also prayed that the eyes of our understanding would be enlightened in the knowledge of Him (see Eph. 1:18-20). As with John's experience of seeing the One seated on the Throne, we all need our own revelation of who Jesus is that is not based on what others are saying. We must know Him for ourselves!

In Matthew 16, Jesus asked His disciples, "Who do men say that I am?" The answers they gave were based on what others were saying about Him. They replied, "Some say John the Baptist; some, Elijah; and others, Jeremiah or one of the prophets." Now, Peter was different; he had received his own personal and deeper revelation from the heavenly Father. He replied, *"Thou art the Christ, the Son of the living God"* (Matt. 16:16). His answer received a powerful and unique response from Jesus. He told Peter, *"Blessed art thou, Simon Barjona: for flesh and blood hath not revealed it unto thee, but my Father which is in heaven"* (Matt. 16:17). In other words, "Peter, you didn't get this revelation or understanding based on hearsay, but from what the Father has personally shown you." In the same way, the stronger our relationship with the One who sits on the Throne, the deeper our revelation of Him becomes—not just of who He is but of the things He shows us.

REVELATION OF THE TRINITY

As believers and those who desire to be used of Him, we must have a healthy understanding of the Trinity. This understanding of the Father, Son, and Holy Spirit will keep us balanced in our revelation and our ability to receive from the Lord.

Let's talk first about having a personal revelation of God the Father. We find this in an important revelation that Jesus presented to Mary when He appeared to her after He'd been resurrected from the dead. Mary had been weeping and mistakenly thought Jesus was a gardener as He appeared to her. However, He reveals something so key for us in our revelation and relationship with Him. In John 20:17 He said, "Don't cling to Me, Mary, as I have not yet ascended to My Father and your Father. My God and your God." Did you notice in this verse the wonderful thing the Lord revealed that is so key for us in our desire to carry and steward Throne Room prophecy? He mentioned to her the characteristics of the Father *before* mentioning His deity as the One who sits on the Throne as Almighty God. Why is this important? It is because we must have a healthy relationship with the Father, knowing Him and His character so we can correctly share His heart. This is why Jesus emphasized God as a Father to Mary first, and *then* He mentioned His deity or power, which speaks of His mighty acts and deeds. When we have a passionate desire and pursuit to know the Father more than just to partake in His display of power or His spiritual gifts, then we will be like Moses who the Bible says *knew God's ways*, meaning His heart, while the children of Israel only knew His acts or displays of power (see Ps. 103:7).

Having a true revelation of your heavenly Father will take you higher in your character, your conduct, and your gifting. It is when we don't have a healthy revelation or relationship with our heavenly Father that prophecies and giftings can become tainted, affecting the pure flow of Heaven through us. This pure flow is always filled with the Father's love and grace, which brings a witness to the words we share. If this is lacking or has not been developed in those who prophesy, then their prophecies, revelations, and delivery can become harsh or even rude. This will be revealed in their words and presentation that can be full of negativity or a spirit of doom and gloom, rather than the heart or Spirit of the Father.

Another thing that happens when the person prophesying doesn't have the proper personal revelation of the Father is they may fall into a tendency to deliver prophetic words that bring up past things in a person's life that have been placed under the blood and forgiven of the Father. Over the years, I have seen some who do this, perhaps out of the need to show validity to their gifting while embarrassing, or even humiliating, the one receiving their words.

This, again, is because they fail to understand the character of the loving heavenly Father who ministers through the covenant of grace and by the blood of His Son.

Lastly, devoid of the revelation of the Father, their prophecies are often laced with a cry for judgment. I will say that not all prophetic words are about promises and blessings, as they may at times carry correction, rebuke, and warning. These words have their place, as long as there is a solid, healthy revelation and relationship with the Father. However, when the one ministering doesn't have that healthy understanding or relationship, the things they prophesy or the spirit in which they speak come from their own unhealthy soul or woundedness. The result is that they minister out of this same spirit or they interpret things through their woundedness rather than through the Spirit of the Father.

Having a healthy relationship with our heavenly Father will enable us to say, as Jesus did, "*he that hath seen me hath seen the Father*" (John 14:9). In addition, we will then be able to say from a healthy spirit and inner soul, "I only do what my Father tells me, or I do what the Father has shown me" (see John 5:19).

Saying that we only do what the Father tells us doesn't mean we don't answer to godly counsel or that our gifting and prophetic words are off-limits to apostolic, prophetic, or pastoral accountability. It doesn't mean that we make ourselves unaccountable to those the Lord puts in our lives as spiritual authority and oversight. When we have strong character, morals, and accountability, it speaks of being properly trained and mentored as true vessels of God, honorably stewarding the gifts we've been given. Always remember, it is a healthy relationship and revelation of your heavenly Father that brings personal character and gifting. It also enables others to identify that our life, character, and gifting are healthy and deeply connected to our Father. When this is in place, we will be able to come up higher, as we mentioned in Chapter One, because we have a teachable spirit that allows for maturity, mentoring, and even correction. God will discipline and correct us as a loving, good Father if we allow it.

> *But you have forgotten that the Scriptures say to God's children, "When the Lord punishes you, don't make light of it, and when he corrects you, don't be discouraged. The Lord corrects the people he loves and disciplines those he calls his own"* (Hebrews 12:5-6 CEV).

It is wise to allow the Lord to have His way and His say in our lives, but it is also wise to have good spiritual fathers and mentors. It was the healthy mentoring, testing, and relationship that Elisha the prophet had with his prophetic mentor Elijah that positioned him to receive a powerful double portion of Elijah's mantle. It is vital for prophetic ministers, regardless of physical or spiritual age, to have a strong relationship with the heavenly Father and with earthly spiritual fathers and mothers as well. I am convinced the Lord does, and will, put the right people in our lives throughout our prophetic journey if we will seek Him first and ask Him.

There are two revelations of Jesus that are important to our spiritual growth as vessels who minister in Throne Room prophecy. We find them in two separate experiences of John's revelation of the Lamb of God. John first saw the Lamb as He had been slain.

> *And I beheld, and, lo, in the midst of the throne and of the four beasts, and in the midst of the elders, stood a Lamb as it had been slain, having seven horns and seven eyes, which are the seven Spirits of God sent forth into all the earth* (Revelation 5:6).

This is the revelation of Jesus who came to earth as fully God and fully man, taking on human flesh to die on the Cross for us all. John's vision gave him a revelation of the crucified Christ, the Lamb who had been slain. Remember the prophetic announcement by John the Baptist when He saw Jesus coming to be baptized? He said, *"Behold, the Lamb of God who takes away the sin of the world!"* (John 1:29 NASB).

John's second revelation came when he saw the resurrected Lamb.

> *Saying with a loud voice, Worthy is the Lamb that was slain to receive power, and riches, and wisdom, and strength, and honour, and glory, and blessing* (Revelation 5:12).

Here, John sees Jesus in a different state. He is clearly seeing the Lamb of God as the resurrected and ascended Christ sitting at the right hand of His Father. These two revelations of the crucified and resurrected Christ make up the foundation of our Christianity and enable us to live healthy spiritual lives. If we are going to minister in Throne Room prophecy, having these two revelations of Jesus is vital.

I want to add another important revelation of Jesus, which we referenced earlier in this chapter—that He is also the giver of the fivefold offices. This means if you are called of Him and stand in these sacred offices, you must choose to be a vessel tried by fire as gold and silver that pays a price for what you have been given by Jesus. You allow Him to shape you, try you, humble you, and reveal the true motives of your heart. God did this with the children of Israel when He led them in the wilderness as He tested and tried them to reveal what was in their hearts, whether they would keep His commands or not (see Deut. 8:2).

When we allow God to take His loving hands and heart and shape us, then we will carry a holy fear, awe, and honor to Him that is void of pride, conceit, self-exaltation of ourselves or giftings. This will carry a testimony that we have gone through the necessary preparation and continuing process of being fashioned by Him in order to stand at a higher level of honor, humility, and fear of the Lord. This enables us to steward the gifts and offices we're given and to be considered vessels of gold, not defiled by cultural mindsets and compromises or with lives not pleasing to His majesty. A healthy revelation of Jesus, the Giver of our gifts, will be the testimony of Him, which always places the focus and glory on Him. This will also be the Spirit of prophecy with which we minister (see Rev. 19:10).

I have heard through many years of ministry people comparing themselves sometimes to certain individuals or prophets of old with regard to their giftings and anointings. Some even claim to have their mantles. We must always remember that mantles—fivefold offices of the apostle, prophet, evangelist, pastor, and teacher—come from Jesus, the Lord of the Church, and not because we want the mantle of someone we admire. *"And he gave some, apostles; and some, prophets; and some, evangelists; and some, pastors and teachers"* (Eph. 4:11). This verse clearly points to the fact that it is *some,* not *all,* who are appointed.

It doesn't come by self-appointment or even by a self-claim to the mantle of someone who once walked the earth. It also doesn't come just because you attend a meeting or a conference that is offering such a thing. In recent times, I have seen such conferences offering to "pray on" the mantle of certain admired figures in the faith, either from the Bible or from more recent times. This simply isn't biblical. I'm not saying there aren't people with legitimate mantles, anointings, or impartations from those who walked powerfully on the earth in the past. That is definitely recognizable in those whose fruit and ministries reveal it. What I want to draw attention to is, rather than always comparing ourselves or comparing others to those who were once used powerfully of the Lord, why not increase our own pursuit, our own understanding and revelation of the Father, Son, and Holy Spirit? This is what Jesus spent His time doing even after the disciples told Him that others were comparing Him to great men of God like Elijah, Jeremiah, and even John the Baptist. Jesus spent time in His ministry revealing His Father, explaining who He was as the Son of God.

It's important to note that Jesus complimented Peter for getting a revelation for himself about who He was. That was to be the primary focus, but the others were comparing Him to great men who'd walked the earth. This, my friend, must also be our emphasis and what dominates our discussion and pursuit—knowing who Jesus is for ourselves!

Lastly, let's talk about the Holy Spirit. We must know who He is and what His function is because we are to be led by Him, submitted to Him, and we must learn to minister alongside Him. This is why the Bible says to let the fellowship of the Holy Spirit be with you all (see 2 Cor. 13:14).

Scripture also tells us the early apostles were submitted to His leading, putting His honor first, before their own agendas or opinions. In Acts 15:28, we're told, *"It seemed good to the Holy Ghost, and to us."* Notice, it was first good or approved by the Holy Spirit first, before the apostles. Many who speak or minister for God are hindered when they are too quick to speak without waiting for the approval or prompting of the Spirit.

True Throne Room prophets are not out to promote themselves, prove their words, or push their gifting through bad behavior. They don't bypass authority or always need to pull people aside before and after church services to "share a word." Prophets and all those who prophesy should not enter churches expecting everyone to notice them and stop what they're doing to heed their prophetic words. In addition, they should guard against elevating themselves as self-appointed prophets in churches or on social media platforms if they are not connected with a good pastor or church in some way.

True Throne Room prophets are disciplined; respectful first of the Holy Spirit, His feelings, and His will; and also to pastors, the church, and others. When they're ministering, they ask themselves, "Should I speak or not? Am I under authority and accountable? Am I the focus—trying to be seen and promoted?" They are first concerned about ministering with the Holy Spirit, who doesn't speak of Himself, but of what He hears from the Father and the Lord of the Church, Jesus Christ.

We can learn a lot from the personality of the Holy Spirit, who doesn't draw attention to Himself. The true anointing and Presence of God come when God is the focal point. This is where the Holy Spirit keeps us in check if we allow Him so that there may be a pure flow of God's words and power through us.

SEVEN LAMPS OF FIRE, SEVEN HORNS, AND SEVEN EYES

It is the Holy Spirit who helps us to develop a heart-to-heart and face-to-face relationship with Him who sits on the Throne. From this intimacy, we move into both a deeper and higher level of ministry to others. We can then say that it is not by our might or power, but by His Spirit (see Zech. 4:6). This partnership with the Holy Spirit is necessary and something He very much wants in the earth. The disciples had this kind of powerful partnership, as the Scripture tells us the Holy Spirit was working with them in powerful healings, signs, wonders, and miracles.

> *And they went forth, and preached every where, the Lord working with them, and confirming the word with signs following. Amen* (Mark 16:20).

Perhaps when John was caught up in the Throne Room, he saw this ministry in the earth—the partnership of the Holy Spirit with the believer. Regular fellowship and dialogue with the Holy Spirit is a key part of this partnership and what every Throne Room prophet must rely on. This is essential in accurately flowing in His true anointing as we exercise prophecy and other gifts of the Spirit. After all, He is the Spirit of Truth, helping us to accurately discern what is of God and what is not!

Let's look at the apostle John's experience in regard to the Holy Spirit and His ministry in the earth that will help deepen our understanding of Him: *"There were seven lamps of fire burning before the throne, which are the seven Spirits of God"* (Rev. 4:5).

What was this that John saw? Are there seven Holy Spirits? Of course not! These were not seven Holy Spirits, but rather representations of His functions as He ministers on the earth.

In order to understand these seven Spirits of God, let's look at the other references to the ministry of the Holy Spirit that John saw in his heavenly encounters. He describes seeing seven Spirits manifested as seven lamps of fire, seven horns, and seven eyes.

Seven lamps of fire: *"and there were seven lamps of fire burning before the throne, which are the seven Spirits of God"* (Rev. 4:5). These are seven dimensions or manifestations of the Spirit. They involve who the Holy Spirit is, the revelation of Him as a person, and His baptism, represented by the fire. We find these seven lamps of fire in Jesus' descriptions of the Holy Spirit in John 14, 15, and 16.

1. The *Comforter* (*Helper*) who will never leave you (John 14:16)

2. The *Spirit of Truth* who will dwell in you and with you (John 14:17)

3. He will *teach* you all things bringing things to remembrance (John 14:26)

4. He will *testify and glorify* Jesus (be a witness, give evidence) (John 15:26; John 16:14)

5. He will *reprove* the world of sin, and of righteousness, and of judgment (John 16:8)

6. He will *guide* you into all truth (John 16:13)

7. He (the *Revealer*) *hears and speaks* to you what He hears and shows you things to come (John 16:13)

And in the midst of the elders, stood a Lamb as it had been slain, having seven horns and seven eyes, which are the seven Spirits of God sent forth into all the earth (Revelation 5:6).

These seven horns of the Lamb represent anointing and power. Horns represent power and were often used when anointing vessels for positions of authority and power. For example, when David was anointed to become king, he was anointed with a horn of oil.

> *And the Lord said unto Samuel, How long wilt thou mourn for Saul, seeing I have rejected him from reigning over Israel? fill thine horn with oil, and go, I will send thee to Jesse the Bethlehemite: for I have provided me a king among his sons* (1 Samuel 16:1).

The Lord chose David and Samuel poured the anointing oil from the horn upon him.

> *Then Samuel took the horn of oil, and anointed him in the midst of his brethren: and the Spirit of the Lord came upon David from that day forward* (1 Samuel 16:13).

These seven horns of the Lamb that were revealed to John also represent the seven "job descriptions" the Lord has given us as believers. Jesus proclaimed Himself as the first one who would minister these things by the anointing of the Holy Spirit. After being tempted of the devil in the wilderness at the start of His ministry, He came out anointed (like with the horn of oil) in the power of the Spirit (see Luke 4:14). He then went into the temple announcing these seven things, describing what He was anointed to do in Luke 4:18.

Luke 4:18-19

1. The Spirit of the Lord is upon me,

2. because he hath anointed me to preach the gospel to the poor;

3. he hath sent me to heal the brokenhearted,

4. to preach deliverance to the captives,

5. and recovering of sight to the blind,

6. to set at liberty them that are bruised,

7. to preach the acceptable year of the Lord.

Jesus had been anointed with the Holy Spirit and with power.

> *How God anointed Jesus of Nazareth with the Holy Ghost and with power: who went about doing good, and healing all that were oppressed of the devil; for God was with him* (Acts 10:38).

Because Jesus was the first to receive this anointing of the Spirit and of power, it is now available to all believers. The Holy Spirit desires us to partner with Him in all seven of these dimensions, releasing His ministry in the earth today!

The seven eyes John describes in the Throne Room are the seven manifestations, or functions, that the Holy Spirit brings to us. For those who are anointed of God, these are listed in our "job description" found in Isaiah 11. They all deal with our ability to receive revelation through our spiritual eyes, represented by the seven eyes of the Lamb.

Isaiah 11:2

1. And the spirit of the Lord shall rest upon him,

2. the spirit of wisdom

3. and understanding,

4. the spirit of counsel

5. and might,

6. the spirit of knowledge

7. and of the fear of the Lord.

These seven attributes of the Holy Spirit are available to all believers, but the level at which we experience them only increases when we choose to put Him first and grow in relationship with Him!

As we can see, these seven lamps, seven horns, and seven eyes are all references to the Holy Spirit's ministry available to the believer. Each of these features can deepen our understanding of who the Holy Spirit is and how He chooses to minister in and through us. As He reveals the Father, He helps us to glorify Jesus and He works in partnership with all those who will yield to Him.

Now that we have discovered the importance of having a healthy and greater knowledge of the Trinity, especially as it relates to Throne Room prophecy, I want to cover another foundational element—it's what I call having the *heart* of the Throne Room!

THE HEART OF THE THRONE ROOM

Having the heart of the Throne Room is making God's heart our primary pursuit and focus. When we carry His heart, it will reflect through the accuracy of the words we speak and our love for others. But how do we really get the heart of the Throne Room? It comes by growing in our love, pursuit, and knowledge of the One seated on the Throne, like the apostle John did. God's heart is what we are after. It is who He is, what He feels, how He thinks, what He likes and dislikes, and what He wants to accomplish in the earth. This is the heart of the Throne Room and must become our heart as well! Not only must we know Him by revelation, but we must be after the things He is after. We need to pursue what is on His heart for every situation. This must be the focus and drive of every true Throne Room prophet and Christian who desires to function in Throne Room prophecy. It is to know the *heart* of Him who is seated on the Throne and, out of great love and respect for Him, to *only* reveal what He desires. This pursuit comes with great hunger, fervor, and passion, where this is your number one goal. Shouldn't our desire be to carry what He feels and what is on His agenda? This only comes as we fear Him or respect what He wants. This is why the Scripture tells us that the secrets of the Lord are with those who fear Him (see Ps. 25:14).

The more we seek to know Him, the more the Lord will open His heart and trust us with the inner places, or His secrets. This depth of relationship always carries a higher level of information, as it is about trust. We must consider His heart first and foremost with whatever it is that He shares with us and whether we are to repeat it, asking Him and ourselves, "Is this something He wants revealed?" This type of respect for the heart of the Throne Room reveals our true intentions and motives to God. It is not self-seeking or promoting, but rather out of the face-to-face relationship that I live, move, and have my being. In other words, as a result of intimacy with Him, I desire a sure word of prophecy that carries the Spirit of Truth that will never bring reproach to Him, the gifting, or the office that He has given. Therefore, I am careful what I share, if I share, and how I share; it is about His heart, His desires, His intent, and not my own.

This should be our standard even if we are not called to an office of the prophet but are prophesying as a believer from time to time. As a believer—a son or a daughter—we are not going to be inconsiderate of the Lord's heart or of others by our lack of discipline, ethics, or etiquette. We want the words that are shared to flow from the pure stream of His heart and to do what the Scripture says regarding prophecy. We want to exhort, edify, and comfort others (see 1 Cor. 14:3). This means we are not pushy, showy, inconsiderate, or demanding as we minister to others. After all, we represent the King, God Himself and His wonderful heart full of words that will be a blessing to others. If we fail to consider God's heart first and then fail to consider the hearts of others, it may cause those who receive prophetic words to despise prophecy or quench, meaning to hinder or stop, the flow of the Holy Spirit. *"Quench not the Spirit. Despise not prophesyings"* (1 Thess. 5:19-20).

This Scripture also means that we are not to despise the gift of prophecy because we may have had a bad experience. It could be that we've received prophetic words from those who have not handled themselves well or perhaps mishandled the prophecy they were giving. In addition, these verses mean that we are not to despise God prophetically communicating His heart through us to others. Despising prophecy would literally mean to bring an unnecessary, inconsiderate viewpoint that touches God deeply in His heart, which leads to the quenching of His Spirit. The reason we must be so careful is, as we mentioned, that genuine prophecy not only considers God's heart but actually *is* God's heart communicated in and through us to others. This is prophecy in its purest manifestation and definition.

Always remember that God's heart is revealed in His written Word, but it is also manifested through prophetic words that express His feelings, His likes and dislikes, His agenda, will, intent, and so on. We should always be asking Him for His heart and aligning ourselves with it. Doing this will bring a higher level of prophetic accuracy, character, conviction, and perspective. It will cause you to pray prayers like, "Lord, I don't want to misrepresent Your heart; put a watch over my mouth and a guard at the door of my lips. I don't want to bring reproach to You or Your name, let alone the sacred gift You have given me. Therefore, let Your heart be heard in and through me as it carries the Spirit of Truth, governed by a sure word of prophecy from my lips."

One day while I was walking my two German Shepherds, the Lord asked me a question that really made an impact on me. I believe our culture often overlooks this, and it is what He is asking today. The Lord said, "My question to you and those in this earth: Does My heart matter?" I stopped at that moment and immediately knew how important this was to the Lord and how often it is not even considered in our day, with the constant arguing and fighting that we see. Has anyone stopped and considered—does God's heart matter? Think about just how sobering that question is. It should make us all stand in awe of Him!

In Noah's day, there was so much corruption and evil that God, as the Scripture declares, repented that He made man and was grieved in His very heart!

> *The Lord saw that humanity had become thoroughly evil on the earth and that every idea their minds thought up was always completely evil. The Lord regretted making human beings on the earth, and he was heartbroken* (Genesis 6:5-6 CEB).

Yet there was one who cared about God and His heart and that was Noah, who walked with Him. *"Noah was a just man and perfect in his generations, and Noah walked with God"* (Gen. 6:9). It was from this revelation of God's heart and His feelings that Noah prophesied a coming flood and an ark of safety. Still, none outside of his family listened because they didn't stop to consider—does God's heart matter?

This is what makes Throne Room prophets unique, as well as those who want to prophesy correctly with God's heart. The heart of God matters to them and they care more about the heart of God than their prophetic words, gifting, or popularity.

Their pursuit of God's heart is what causes the words they've been given by the Lord to carry greater accuracy and authority when they are spoken. Their focus is not on speaking from a platform; rather, it is on the One seated on the Throne, as it was with the apostle John when he was caught up to the Throne Room: *"and one sat on the throne"* (Rev. 4:2).

John was captivated by the One who sits on the Throne; he was so deeply impacted that he fell on his face as a dead man. *"And when I saw him, I fell at his feet as dead"* (Rev. 1:17). That is the best place and position for receiving the heart of the Lord—on our face before Him!

The heart of the Throne Room will keep our motives and focus in check and in proper alignment, where the focus is not on us but on the Lord! Sadly, this is often where the young and immature, and sometimes even those who have ministered for the Lord for many years, get off track. We must be reminded that it is not about how powerful we are or how much people sing our praises. It must always be about Him who sits on the Throne. No gift, no unction, no revelation given, and no person can truly function correctly without Him. Where He becomes grieved is when we spend our time promoting ourselves, our gifts, our ministries, or our prophetic words and bragging about the number of results we see.

Let's talk about numbers for a moment. In this current media-driven culture, it's easy to get caught up in numbers, thinking that they prove our success. There certainly is a place for letting viewers online see the size of crowds at an event or hear testimonies of miracles that occur through our ministries. This can also include the number of those saved, baptized, healed, and so on. While sharing the great things the Lord does through the ministry we are called to, we also need to be careful that we aren't drawing attention to ourselves and our own successes in ministry to the point that it draws attention away from the Lord.

Now, we understand the Book of Acts speaks of the number of souls saved and the size of the crowds, but let's consider something for a moment in context of these numbers. The author of the Book of Acts, when referencing how many were saved, filled with Spirit, or healed, never spoke from a spirit of pride, comparison, or self-promotion that fills much of today's culture. This self-centeredness has also now, at times, crept into the Church. When sharing our successes, we should always strive to draw attention to the Spirit of God working through His Church to bring witness or validity to the resurrected Christ and not to ourselves. Also, when Jesus was speaking to the seven churches in Revelation as He was exhorting, instructing, and even rebuking them, He never even mentioned, not even once, any statistics concerning the size of their churches. Instead, His message was directed toward their character and obedience.

Understanding this helps us to remember that the call from the One from the Throne Room is to bring all focus and attention on Him and not on us. Let's continue to bring honor to Him as we humbly let others know how He is using us. This will cause a beautiful, pure flow of God's heart *to* you and then powerfully *through* you! The Holy Spirit in us, for us, and through us will greatly increase and manifest in our lives and ministry. God's heart *does* matter, and as we keep this in mind, we will be pure vessels that allow His heart to flow freely to those around us.

FACE TO FACE, HEART TO HEART, AND MOUTH TO MOUTH

As we come to the end of this chapter, I want to review what we have discussed thus far. First, we have looked at the importance of the Throne Room, followed by the importance of establishing our focus upon the One seated on the Throne. We discovered that when the One seated on the Throne is our pursuit and passion, the ministry of the Holy Spirit is manifested more powerfully.

I want to give you one final thought that will cause the prophetic to become even more precise and accurate. It's what happens when we establish face-to-face, heart-to-heart encounters with Him like the apostle John had. We may never have encounters at John's level, but we can certainly have our own!

Moses had this wonderful heart-to-heart, face-to-face, mouth-to-mouth relationship with God.

And Moses said unto the Lord, O my Lord, I am not eloquent, neither heretofore, nor since thou hast spoken unto thy servant: but I am slow of speech, and of a slow tongue. And the Lord said unto him, Who hath made man's mouth? or who maketh the dumb, or deaf, or the seeing, or the blind? have not

I the Lord? Now therefore go, and I will be with thy mouth, and teach thee what thou shalt say (Exodus 4:10-12).

Throne Room prophets—and really, every believer—must always be about intimate relationship with God as Moses was.

And the Lord spake unto Moses face to face, as a man speaketh unto his friend (Exodus 33:11).

This level of relationship requires heart-to-heart talks with God where we hear His heart, know His feelings, ask Him questions, and wait for Him to answer. It is about dialogues, not just monologues! This is what the Lord intended when He made man, as we can see with Adam and Eve and how they walked with God, conversing with Him in relationship. It is also what we see with Enoch, who walked with God and was taken up by God. *"And Enoch walked with God: and he was not; for God took him"* (Gen. 5:24). In other words, Enoch had reached such a level of intimate relationship with Lord that God took him where He was.

There are spiritual places, even levels, where the Lord takes those whose pursuit of Him is more important than the pursuit of title, position, or platform. Let everything we do come from our deep conversations and time with God! Spending time with God is freedom to converse, discuss things, and enjoy one another's company. I have often designated a chair where the Lord can come and sit with me, and I speak to Him as if I literally see Him with my fleshly eyes. Now this may sound strange, but I have learned the more real I make Him, the more real He becomes in my life. I am not afraid to ask Him questions and then wait for an answer. I mean hard questions that I can't figure out on my own—things I want to know, that speak of Him and reveal His character to me.

I remember a time I wanted to really step up my time and increase my prayer commitment to the Lord. I determined that I was going to start getting up every morning even earlier than I already had been. I set my alarm and awoke before the birds were singing and began to pray. I stumbled through my words, drifting in and out of sleep. I even tried changing my prayer position to every possible way you can imagine in my attempt to stay awake. I fell asleep and woke up only to see that I had been drooling as I dozed off! I started to feel really bad about falling asleep in His presence and thinking I was no better than the disciples who did the same in the Garden of Gethsemane. When I heard the Lord speak to me, He said, "Hank, why don't you go back to bed and get some rest and come back when we both will enjoy this!"

What? Wait, you mean I can go back to bed? It was then that I realized that He wants to enjoy the time we spend together, and He saw that my heart was right in pursuing Him. However, pursuing Him is not to be based on self-imposed rules that take the joy of the relationship out of focus.

Now I am certainly not saying that we shouldn't press ourselves in prayer and avoid sleeping at times. There are times of intercession when we must stay awake and press strongly and fervently in prayer because we are praying urgently for someone or something else. When Jesus found His disciples sleeping, He *did* ask if they could not even pray with Him for one hour. However, these times of intercession are different and are not necessarily about us developing intimacy and dialogue with the Lord. I am speaking of a relationship that requires understanding from those involved. God knows I do pray consistently, and I like doing so. He noticed and even appreciated my hunger. But I also believe He understood how much I needed to rest and to come back when we could have more enjoyable and meaningful fellowship.

What I am wanting to draw attention to is the need for relationship with Him. It is so vital for our walk and sharpens our ability to hear and receive from Him. It is from this relationship that the pure stream from God's heart to our heart flows into our mouths and through our lips. One such example that we can prophetically apply to our lives is seen when Elisha prayed for the Shunamite woman's young child who had died. Remember, this was the very child he had prophesied would be born to break the barrenness of her womb, and now the child had fallen sick and died!

Elisha performed three prophetic acts that we can apply to aid us in our prophetic accuracy. The story also reveals the three primary ways that God communicates to us by our seeing, hearing, and feeling (or perceiving).

> *And he went up, and lay upon the child, and put his mouth upon his mouth, and his eyes upon his eyes, and his hands upon his hands: and stretched himself upon the child; and the flesh of the child waxed warm. Then he returned, and walked in the*

> *house to and fro; and went up, and stretched him-*
> *self upon him: and the child sneezed seven times,*
> *and the child opened his eyes* (2 Kings 4:34-35).

Elisha first put his mouth upon the young child's mouth, showing us how the Lord puts His prophetic words in our mouths so we may speak as His voice in the earth. As God's Spirit is upon us, He breathes the inspiration of His heart to us. It is a beautiful prophetic picture of how God's words are given to us and to others through prophecy. It also shows us that He communicates to us by something we hear, as we hear the prophetic words that are spoken.

Second, Elisha put his eyes upon the child's eyes, representing how the Lord communicates by something we see. This also reminds us that the prophetic ministry is a "seeing ministry." He will speak to us through visions, dreams, and revelations, bringing pictures to our spirits.

Third, Elisha put his hands upon this child's hands, which reminds us that all prophets are servants. We represent the ministry of serving when sharing the secrets of the Lord. Remember, the secrets of God belong to His *servants* the prophets as stated in Amos 3:7. It also reminds us that we are His hands and heart extended in the earth. This prophetic act also shows us, again, how God communicates to us by things we will prophetically feel or perceive from our times with Him.

Elisha's prophetic acts show us the role and function that the prophetic ministry should have as one of the foundational ministries in the earth today. Without the prophetic, we as well as churches can become lifeless like this child, never coming to maturity. It took the prophetic ministry to bring this child into his destiny. We need the prophetic ministry today in the same way, causing people and churches to reach their full potential and maturity.

Elisha stretched himself forth upon the child, showing us that the prophetic ministry is meant for the whole Body of Christ. When the prophetic is ministered in the right spirit, it will revitalize and "reheat" the Body of Christ just as this child's body was warmed and revived. When prophets and prophecy flow correctly, it will give and bring life to individuals, churches, cities, governments, and nations!

There is an important key in John's encounter that unlocks the heart of God to speak to us face to face, heart to heart, and mouth to mouth. Notice when John received this call to come higher it wasn't until *after* something.

> *After this I looked, and, behold, a door was opened in heaven: and the first voice which I heard was as it were of a trumpet talking with me; which said, Come up hither, and I will shew thee things which must be hereafter* (Revelation 4:1).

His call to come up higher and the prophetic upgrade he experienced came *after* there was a revelation given him and mention of the key of David in Revelation 3. Here it's revealed that Jesus holds this key that opens doors. These "doors" also include our hearts and the hearts of those we speak to prophetically.

And to the angel of the church in Philadelphia write; These things saith he that is holy, he that is true, he that hath the key of David, he that openeth, and no man shutteth; and shutteth, and no man openeth (Revelation 3:7).

This key of David unlocks the door of the human heart, not only to receive the Lord but to also hear from Him. It is the very thing that causes us to have a more intimate relationship and go deeper with Him. This key is this face-to-face, heart-to-heart, and mouth-to-mouth relationship with the Living God that we are speaking about!

Behold, I stand at the door, and knock: if any man hear my voice, and open the door, I will come in to him, and will sup with him, and he with me (Revelation 3:20).

We can't truly go to another level or come up higher until we have this key to all gifting, anointing, and function—intimacy with the Lord! David was a man after God's own heart, and so must we be.

And when he had removed him, he raised up unto them David to be their king; to whom also he gave their testimony, and said, I have found David the son of Jesse, a man after mine own heart, which shall fulfil all my will (Acts 13:22).

God didn't call David a man after His prophetic revelation or words, even though those are evident in genuine prophetic ministry; He called David a man after His *heart.* Prophetic revelation comes as a result of seeking the Lord's heart. Let's make that our passion and our pursuit as well!

May this be our heart cry today—to truly know Him and His beautiful heart! When we live from this place, we will definitely see the upgrade that He brings to our lives, anointings, giftings, and ministries. I encourage you to take hold of that key of David and unlock His secrets, revelations, prophetic insights, and fellowship that will change you! When you do, get ready for a pure flow from His heart to your heart. His face will be before your face and His beautiful words will flow through your mouth, carrying and declaring the very heart of the Throne Room!

Chapter Three

THRONE ROOM PROPHETS AND PROPHECY

*"Come up here, and I will show you
what must take place after this."*
—Revelation 4:1, NIV

In my very early years of walking with the Lord, a pastor asked me what I was called to do in the ministry. This pastor was asking what ministry office I felt called to, so in the best way I knew I tried to tell them. I answered, "I know God uses me as an evangelist; I am seeing many saved on the streets and other places, but I also believe I am called to the prophetic office." Of course, at the time I had limited understanding of the prophet's office, but I was already seeing the anointing for it manifest in my life.

However, the response from this pastor caught me off guard. They pointed their finger at me and in a very opposing manner said, "No, you are not a prophet, you are an evangelist!" Those words went deep into my heart and caused a great sense of discouragement and confusion. I really had felt that I was called to be a prophet and that is what God was asking me to do for Him. I even reminded myself of the Throne Room experience when I had been filled with the Holy Spirit; that was when my call had been deposited in me. I'd never told anyone but my wife Brenda that I had felt called to the prophetic office.

One thing that experience taught me is that we need to be careful who we share our dreams and giftings with. Remember, it cost Joseph a lot of hardship and heartbreak when he shared his dream with his jealous brothers. I've learned that you don't have to go around telling everyone that you are a prophet or pushing yourself to open doors of opportunity. I am glad to have learned this early on.

When called to be a prophet, one does not have tell everyone what their title is. This is because being a prophet of the Lord is not just a title; it's a ministry function. It is also a spiritual office given by Jesus, the Lord of the Church. If one is truly called to be a prophet, there will be fruit that will support what they have been called to do. It is far better and more honorable to display the fruit of our character and our lives and let the gifting entrusted to us testify of what we are called to do. No matter what Jesus has entrusted us with, we must remain humbled by His calling and remind ourselves that it is an honor to represent Him.

We have to be confident in what the Lord has called us to do and remain strong in our character, because as we mentioned previously, the calling of a prophet does not come without misunderstanding and even persecution at times. If we are going to function as prophetic ministers, we must be prepared for this. Naturally, every ministry gift will at times be misspoken about, and that comes with the territory of being in ministry, period. Really, it comes with the territory for simply being a believer because the Gospel tells us to expect persecution.

> *Yea, and all that will live godly in Christ Jesus shall suffer persecution* (2 Timothy 3:12).

However, I do believe it gets heightened in the prophetic because people have unique expectations of that office. Most people want those in the prophetic office to be flawless and unable to make a mistake. We will talk more about perfect accuracy in Chapter Five, but it's important that we learn how to respond to the critics who come with the prophetic office. The more we are grounded in relationship with the Lord and spend consistent time with Him, the more we'll be able to stay in love and forgiveness and exercise wisdom, not listening too much to what people say, whether compliments or critiques.

I did my best to keep my heart right in regard to the disagreement and opposition from the pastor who told me they didn't believe I was called to be a prophet, but it was a process. The enemy used that to try and keep me from moving toward my calling. From that experience, as a pastor I also realize I must be careful not to dismiss the call a person may feel on their life, whether I see it or not. I need to help guide them, but not dismiss them altogether, as that can deeply discourage people from walking in what the Lord wants for them.

I am confident that walking through that situation is what brought the Lord's confirmation to me through the many prophetic utterances that would come in the following years. God was faithful to ensure that one word spoken by that pastor wasn't going to be the final word. He began to bring countless other voices into our lives that confirmed my prophetic calling and eventually the truth caused that pastor's words to be uprooted from my heart.

I began to understand that I was, in fact, hearing correctly regarding the prophetic office and ministry call upon my life. I will never forget the day when my wife and I received a word from a very seasoned veteran in the prophetic ministry. He said, "Hank and Brenda, the Lord is calling you both and will use you both as prophets all over the world and it will be to the highest of nations, to the lowest of nations, to those who are well known, and even to those no one knows about. God is changing your feathers from chicken feathers to duck feathers—their words and what they say will roll off your backs like ducks' feathers so you can be bold and confident with the word of the Lord."

This word not only confirmed the calling that we felt but also helped us to better understand the importance of letting the Lord make and mold us, so we can have the character to stand against opposition and criticism that may arise at times. This is a great example of how when someone is called to be a Throne Room prophet they need the company of prophets and others in their lives to encourage them and bounce things off of, as we see in Scripture. In First Samuel 10, we see how the company of prophets were hanging out together. I'm not saying we should just find people who agree with everything we say and do. Rather, I'm saying there is fellowship, agreement, revelation, and encouragement in the company of others who understand and desire the word of the Lord. It also reminds us that we must remain teachable so the Lord can continue to develop needed character, tweaking our fortitude through those we surround ourselves with.

I believe this has greatly aided my wife and I in our ministries. We've been surrounded by seasoned vessels, many generals in the faith; we also have had good pastors and spiritual fathers we could open our hearts and lives to, who have helped us in the calling entrusted to us. Having godly counsel and authority will help us to be honest and humble enough to realize we are all undone without God and we all need His continual working in our lives. Not one of us has arrived; we are all a work in process for the Lord.

In the years that followed this significant prophetic word, God was faithful to keep undergirding the prophetic call on our lives. We didn't ask for it, but He saw to it because the call was genuine. My wife, Brenda, and I, no matter what meeting we attended in our early years of ministry, seemed to get called out of the audience and prophesied to. Those prophetic words over us kept confirming the call to the prophetic ministry and office. These prophecies came consistently in a series after the incident I opened this chapter with, but there was one specific prophecy that forever changed us and marked our life and ministry. We received a word from a woman who was speaking at an event we attended; she walked up to us during the service and began to prophesy. She spoke about us being called to teach and minister the word of God. She then pointed at me, declaring I was called to be a prophet for the Lord. She continued, "How low are you willing to bow to see how high I will raise you? says the Lord." In other words, she was prophesying the only way up would be down—down on my knees and in a place of humility. I thank God for those words as they have been a continual reminder for Brenda and me of our true focus, character, and commitment to God and our calling.

I want to take a moment to encourage you that if you are called to be a prophet, God will not let that fail. You don't have to force it, just be obedient. If your call is genuine and from Heaven, God will make sure it is not aborted. It doesn't matter who doesn't believe in you or who the enemy uses to try to discourage you. Even well-meaning people can be used to discourage us without realizing it, as in my case, but the Lord ensured that the ministry call came forth. Rest in that and know if you are called to be a prophet, God will make it happen! Just stay humble and let the Lord do the work.

That said, what marks genuine prophets or prophetic vessels is humility. They will carry this quality and a presence that marks them and identifies them as those who have been with the Lord. A true Throne Room prophet is one who serves with their title and gifting, recognizing it is a function with which to serve the Lord and others as He directs. *"Surely the Lord God will do nothing, but he revealeth his secret unto his servants the prophets"* (Amos 3:7). I have heard this Scripture spoken in reference to the Lord always keeping the prophets informed first before He does anything in the earth. While that is true, it important to note this is not the only truth found in this verse. Notice how it says, *"his servants the prophets."* We must be reminded of the One whom we serve and the awesome responsibility to carry His words and revelation as His servants. Our prophetic calling is one of serving, not of being served.

I believe the word I heard from the Lord, when He asked how low we were willing to bow, can be applied to us all. How low are we really willing to bow and humble ourselves to see how high He will raise us as His prophetic servants? As I have been saying, this means we don't have to push and make a place for ourselves. We just need to be servants in the Kingdom and let God do the rest.

As we are intentional about humbling ourselves, the presence of God will mark our lives and ministries. It was not hard for people to see that the disciples had spent time with Jesus because they carried His presence, which was manifested through signs, wonders, and mighty deeds. This presence comes when there is a life of serving in purity, integrity, and strong character. These qualities can be easily found in our speech, conduct, morals, methods, message, money handling, marriage, and family to name a few. Jesus reminded us why He came, which needs to be our standard and example as well. He told us that He didn't come to *be* served, but rather to serve. In fact, the apostle Paul describes Jesus as one whom no man who ever walked this planet could match in their character, gifting, revelation, glory, anointing, signs, wonders, and healings.

Jesus was often demonstrative, but He wasn't a showman or even the least bit arrogant in His methods or ministry. Look at what Paul says about how the Lord walked on this earth and how He ministered. This needs to be our standard.

> *But made himself of no reputation, and took upon him the form of a servant, and was made in the likeness of men: and being found in fashion as a man, he humbled himself, and became obedient unto death, even the death of the cross* (Philippians 2:7-8).

Did you notice how He humbled Himself and did not come to build His own reputation but came as a servant to God His Father and others? His attitude and servant's heart were, "Whatever You want, God, that is what I will do." Jesus said, "I am here to do what My Father has shown me, and I speak what He has told me" (see John 5:19). Jesus could say that because He was as a son under authority and accountability. He was not only submitted to God the Father but operated in submission to human authority as well.

We can learn a lot from Him when He submitted His first miracle of water into wine and offered it to the governor of the feast. In other words, He didn't take over or draw attention to His own ministry, but instead He submitted it to the one in charge. This is an example for us, that we would take on the same humble servant's approach as Jesus. In Jesus' case, He submitted the wine (representative of the anointing) to the person in charge.

This also teaches those of us who minister prophetically that we always submit our gifts to those in charge. For example, if we are visiting or even invited as a guest speaker in another pastor's church, we must submit to their authority, being respectful of protocol, timelines, and mindful of how that pastor functions. If we are visiting or attending a church, not as a guest speaker, we should not go around ministering to people in the church. Remember, the pastor is the governor in charge of the feast, so to speak. Jesus displayed this kind of attitude of honor because He spent much time in prayer with His Father, being molded in His presence.

CHANGED AND SHAPED IN HIS PRESENCE

Like Jesus, in order to receive the heart of God and the right attitude in ministering to others, we must spend time with the Lord. Being developed for ministry is a lifelong process. This will require many encounters in the Throne Room, pouring our hearts out to Him and letting Him make us into exactly what He wants. No matter how much God promotes us and uses us, we have to remain pliable and teachable. Doing this also means we have a willingness to recognize our imperfections and work on these areas as the Holy Spirit shows them to us.

We definitely need strong giftings today, but they must be coupled with strong development of character, protocol, and mentoring. So many today have strong giftings but are underdeveloped in their character. Again, this is often due to lack of good spiritual mentors, no local church connection, or simply because of independent, unaccountable mindsets.

As a result, some with genuine gifts never see them come to proper fruition. Having our foundations set deeply is so vital to seeing our gifts and callings become effective. I know some people will always say, "But I can't seem to find a pastor who understands my call!" That may be true, but consider that perhaps our pastor isn't necessarily required to "understand" our call. What I mean is, when we attend a church and submit to its leadership, we are there not to primarily grow our ministry or calling. We are there to grow as *believers* and learn how to serve the church and function alongside others in the Kingdom. We learn manners, ethics, and servanthood. In our local church, we are there to help the wider vision of that church's mission, not to build our own. From that, God will ensure every genuinely called person gets what they need from the growth opportunities the local church environment provides. Even if your local church doesn't have any formal training for what you feel called to do, prophetic or otherwise, many training courses and online schools can help with this. We can't expect pastors to be required to ensure the proper training for every person's specific calling.

The key is, we need to continually have the foundation of a local church body and mentors in our lives. If many who have been called to the prophetic had their foundations set deeply in this manner, allowing for proper mentoring and input, they would now be better equipped. Their ministries would be better represented, without reproach and also better prepared to endure for the long haul.

Let's look once again at the prophet Isaiah as an example of what makes a prophet, and all believers who prophesy, genuine. It is worth delving deeper into because Isaiah's experience is vital. He had an encounter with the Lord that forever changed him and caused his outlook and motive to change. We see this in Isaiah 6:

> *Then said I, Woe is me! for I am undone; because I am a man of unclean lips, and I dwell in the midst of a people of unclean lips: for mine eyes have seen the King, the Lord of hosts* (Isaiah 6:5).

When Isaiah truly came into revelation of who God is, it was followed by his cry of *"woe is me."* After he saw the King, the Lord of Hosts, he made this cry of being undone and a man of unclean lips. Consider for a moment how the attention shifted from Isaiah's prophetic office, anointing, and function to his own human weakness and frailty in the presence of the Lord. This is evident by the six previous "woes" that he'd spoken prophetically in Isaiah 5. He prophesied from his prophetic office and anointing concerning the greedy and those whose lifestyles were consumed with partying. He prophesied woe to the mockers of God, to the sexually perverted, the conceited, and to those who practiced lawlessness. It was "woe unto *them*" as he pointed out their shortcomings. Yet now, after being in the Throne Room, it wasn't about *them* but his *own* shortcomings as he says, "Woe is *me!*" This is his response as he recognizes his call to be a prophet, and the words with which he was entrusted were nothing compared to the Giver of his office and gifting, the Lord Jesus Christ! It caused him to take the attention off his gifting and message to others and look at his own life as the messenger.

This is a beautiful picture of the making of a prophet as they must be changed by and in His presence. They must be molded and made by Him, allowing the Lord to refine them so they may stand as vessels of honor. Only then are we truly prepared and changed, where we realize nothing is as important or greater than Him. Isaiah came to that realization. This is a realization every Throne Room prophet must have as well.

We can learn from Isaiah's encounter with the Lord that in order to effectively minister for Him in whatever facet that may be, we need to allow God to mold us, change us, and purify us first. If we bypass this necessary process, it will put the prophet's attention more on the need for others to change than ourselves. We will spend our time saying, "woe unto them" rather than looking inward at our own need to be continually changed by and in His presence. When this change happens first in us, then the assignment given by the Lord to prophesy words that call for change, repentance, and correction will be ministered in the right spirit. This is because we have been purified, our lips cleansed, and we recognize our own frailty outside of His grace. This becomes the spirit, the revelation, and the position we minister from, just like we see with Isaiah. This is the call that the Lord is extending at this time, and it's what marks a true, genuine prophet today.

Consider for a moment those in Scripture who had the same feeling and experience of being completely undone in His presence like Isaiah. Remember Peter, who fell down at Jesus' feet, asking that He would depart from him because he knew his own sinful human state. And we see Job, whom the Scripture declares abhorred himself and repented in dust and ashes. *"So I hate the things that I have said. And I put dust and ashes on myself to show how sorry I am"* (Job 42:6 NLV). How about Moses, who hid his face because he was afraid to look upon God? (See Exodus 3:6.)

In all these examples, we can conclude that their own human weakness was magnified and became evident when they encountered the Lord's awesome presence. It's not self-condemnation but rather self-examination that empties us to be more like Him. This self-examination will aid us in carrying the word of the Lord inside us with the right spirit. Once we empty ourselves, He can fill us and use us in a supernatural, powerful way that reflects Him.

We see another prophetic example of this, again from the first miracle of Jesus. He had the wedding guests of Cana fill six empty water pots with water. This speaks prophetically of salvation that only comes through Jesus Christ. The empty pots represent the condition of mankind without God—we are empty and in need of His presence. The contents of these pots were supernaturally transformed when Jesus turned the water into new wine. This transformation of the water into wine is not only a prophetic type of the Holy Spirit, who baptizes and fills us after our salvation (see Acts 2), but it is also what happens to us when we choose to empty ourselves to be used of Him. God's presence and the new wine of the Holy Spirit are always available to us when we empty ourselves before Him! This is what happened to the believers in Acts 2 when they were filled with the new wine of the Holy Spirit.

Like the empty water pots, Isaiah was supernaturally transformed by the Lord's presence as he humbled and emptied himself before the Lord. As a result, he also gained a true prophetic revelation and insight into the condition of the people he was prophesying to.

> *And he laid it upon my mouth, and said, Lo, this hath touched thy lips; and thine iniquity is taken away, and thy sin purged. Also I heard the voice of the Lord, saying, Whom shall I send, and who will go for us? Then said I, Here am I; send me. And he said, Go, and tell this people, Hear ye indeed, but understand not; and see ye indeed, but perceive not* (Isaiah 6:7-9).

Once Isaiah's lips had been touched by being in the presence of God and his iniquity was taken away and his sin purged, he was then ready to be sent by the Lord to speak His words. When this is out of order in prophetic vessels, it can cause us to spend more time focusing on the words *we* prophesy, rather than allowing those words to form in us through the power of His presence. We should never allow our desire to be used of the Lord to be greater than our desire to be changed by the Lord. The more we are changed in His presence, the more He can use us and the more effectively our words will touch others. It also helps us in making necessary changes that better us and position us to have the right heart, motives, character, and focus. Our lips will be marked like Isaiah's, with Heaven's touch and fire that will be felt and heard in the words we prophesy!

Once we understand that there is a holy fire that is taken from His altar to purify and cleanse us, it will help us to better speak His words and not our own. It is important to spend time with Him consistently and never forget that the Throne is for God—that is where He rules and reigns, and it is the place of our determined pursuit. The altar, however, is for us—so we may find cleansing, purging, and the surrender of our lives and wills to Him.

There is such a glorious change that happens from being in His presence, especially when we worship. Look at what happened to the twenty-four elders when they worshiped the Lord.

> *The four and twenty elders fall down before him that sat on the throne, and worship him that liveth for ever and ever, and cast their crowns before the throne, saying, Thou art worthy, O Lord, to receive glory and honour and power* (Revelation 4:10-11).

In order to fall down, they must have been sitting or standing, which means they had to make a heartfelt commitment and connection to bow before the Lord. It wasn't about their crowned positions, titles, or functions—it was about focusing on and worshiping God. The same is true for us and will also enable us to correctly minister to others. We will be prepared like the apostle John to come up higher and see the things that will "come hereafter," or in the future. In other words, our heartfelt commitment and decision to come into His presence will sharpen our spiritual senses and position us like John to go higher in the prophetic and prophesy change to others.

I WILL SHOW *YOU* THINGS

When John was caught up to the Throne Room, as we mentioned, he was told that the Lord would show him things that would come hereafter. *"Come up hither, and I will shew thee things which must be hereafter"* (Rev. 4:1).

I want you to notice the emphasis on "show *you*," meaning God desires to show us things personally that will take place in our lives, in the lives of others, and in the earth. In other words, God did and still does choose to reveal His secrets to mankind and entrusts us to speak for Him. This is why He has set prophets in His Church today (see 1 Cor. 12:28). It is also why prophecy has been given to every generation since the time Peter declared on the day of Pentecost that our sons and daughters would prophesy (see Acts 2:17).

You don't have to be a prophet or have a prophetic gift to hear from the Lord. That is why the Scripture repeats the phrase in the New Testament at least fifteen times, "Let those that have ears to hear, hear what the Spirit is saying." This is not just talking about our natural ears, but it is speaking of our spiritual ears. We can learn to sharpen these spiritual ears so that we recognize the voice of the Lord more clearly. This is done by staying in His presence, praying, and studying His Word.

This is exactly what happened with the young prophet Samuel, which shows us that God will talk to us at any age. He heard the voice because he laid down next to the ark of the covenant, which was the presence of the Lord. Samuel was connected to the things of God.

> *The lamp of God had not yet gone out, and Samuel*
> *was lying down in the house of the Lord, where*
> *the ark of God was. Then the Lord called Samuel*
> (1 Samuel 3:3-4 NIV).

Now, the priest Eli didn't hear the Lord because rather than lying down in the presence of God, he instead lay down, as the Scripture says, in his own place, or "in his usual place." *"One night Eli, whose eyes were becoming so weak that he could barely see, was lying down in his usual place"* (1 Sam. 3:2 NIV). This means he resorted to his own place of comfort and choice, which was not the presence of God. Did you notice Eli's condition? The weakness of his eyes speaks of his inability to discern the word of the Lord. His spiritual and natural senses were affected because he didn't spend time in the presence of God, which was where the ark of the covenant was. Instead, he lay down in his usual place, separate from the Lord's presence. We need to be wise not to get stuck in habits, our usual routines, or busy schedules that cause us to not spend time with the Lord. This is especially true for those called to the office of prophet because so much of their gifting requires time in His presence to accurately communicate the Lord's heart. When this is hindered, interrupted, or not a priority, it will hinder hearing and receiving from the Lord, like it did with Eli the priest. His eyes became weak, meaning he wasn't sharp in his perception and discernment. This is the same for us as our own spiritual senses and prophetic flow and discernment will be hindered if we neglect being in the place of the Lord. Eli didn't hear God's voice because he was spending time in his usual place or routine. Instead, the voice of the Lord came to young Samuel, who was in the presence of God!

If you want to sharpen your hearing, your spiritual perception, and release more accurate flow of prophecy, be wise to choose the place of His presence like Samuel did, and not the usual place of Eli. When you do, He will show *you*, just as He showed the apostle John, prophetic revelation of things.

Let's consider another way to position ourselves to hear the Lord's voice. Elijah was a strong prophet who heard the voice of the Lord. When the widow's son died, he performed a prophetic act, raising the boy back to life. This act can be prophetically applied to us, whether we are a prophet or a believer who prophesies. Notice what he did to develop a greater sensitivity to the Lord and be received and recognized as a true Throne Room prophet. Elijah would be considered a true Throne Room prophet as his life and ministry had great impact upon the time he lived and even today we can glean insights from him.

He did three things that are essential for Throne Room prophets and those who want to come up higher in the things of God and increase prophetic accuracy.

> *And he stretched himself upon the child three times, and cried unto the Lord, and said, O Lord my God, I pray thee, let this child's soul come into him again. And the Lord heard the voice of Elijah; and the soul of the child came into him again, and he revived* (1 Kings 17:21-22).

1. In verse 21, *"he cried unto the Lord."* You have to set a time and place to seek the Lord with all your heart and might. We must learn to press into God.

2. Then, *"he stretched himself upon the child."* We need to be willing to stretch ourselves and be willing to learn to prophesy and stretch our spiritual hearing.

3. Again in verse 21, *"three times."* Remember, don't quit or give up. Keep trying more than once, as each time you will go higher!

We must remember that there are many ways in which God speaks today that qualify as true Throne Room prophecy. It doesn't have to be you putting a hand on someone and saying, "Thus saith the Lord," for it to be considered Throne Room prophecy. Remember, prophecy is God's heart, mind, will, intent, and agenda revealed. This can come through various means or ways that the Lord communicates to us today.

There are different ways in which the Lord communicates His heart through Throne Room prophecy. He may choose to communicate through something we see, hear, or perceive. It may be through visions, dreams, thoughts, impressions, gut feelings, repeated messages, or just everyday life events. The key is to know He is speaking and communicating more than we realize.

Yet I have still found in all the various ways the Lord speaks to us, the primary way is by the inward witness of His voice, or that still small voice that speaks to us. We see this with the prophet Elijah. Much like us, he was wanting to discern the voice of the Lord, but the Lord's voice was not in the things he expected. The Lord was not in the wind, the fire, or the shaking, but in the still small voice (see 1 Kings 19:12). All three of these ways—the wind, fire, and shakings—represent how God communicates through things we see, hear, or feel. But the Lord used the still small voice to get Elijah's attention.

Elijah had to accurately discern whether God was speaking in the wind, the fire, and the shaking. Many times, we do the same thing as Elijah when it comes to hearing the Lord—we expect His voice in the obvious rather than in the quiet, unseen things. We must remember that God does sometimes speak in the wind, fire, and shakings. Yet every prophetic vessel, especially the Throne Room prophet, must learn how to correctly hear and discern the voice of the Lord.

We can learn some things about hearing God and delivering prophecy from the wind, the fire, and the shaking in Elijah's story. What do they represent and how should they be discerned when hearing the word of the Lord?

First, the prophet must not always treat the word of the Lord, their gifting or anointing, like the wind. The wind can have a mysterious way about it—you can't see it, but you can hear it, feel it, and see its effects. In the same way, our gifting and anointing may be powerful, but not every prophecy has to be a "super-spiritual," mysterious phenomenon that blows everyone away and causes the hearer to look at us rather than Jesus.

Second, the Throne Room prophet must not always be quick to want to call down fire like James and John were.

Remember that Jesus rebuked them for not knowing what spirit they were of. Prophets and people speaking prophetically who call down fire, seeing only the bad and portraying God as angry and judgmental, often don't know what spirit they are speaking from. When we hear a prophetic vessel or prophet constantly call down fire and judgment, we need to be aware that perhaps the words they are prophesying are out of balance. This can be because the person prophesying might be speaking from their own fire of revelation and is not correctly communicating the heart, mind, will, and intent of the Lord. Their own spirit or perspective could be tainted in some way. This is where Jonah got off course and where immature prophets often make the same mistake. They lean toward consistently prophesying words of destruction, vengeance, and God's judgments. When God chooses not to manifest according to their heated prophecies, they get mad like Jonah did and adopt a wrong attitude instead of adjusting themselves.

Third, the prophet must not always feel the need to give an earth-shaking or Heaven-shaking prophecy that gains them attention and popularity. Again, this is why some are not hearing the Lord's still small voice, which equally carries Throne Room authority and accuracy. Instead they are driven to only look for the fiery, mysterious, or earth-shaking way that God may speak or manifest.

The key thing we must remember is that the Lord desires to show you and I things that carry prophetic truth and revelation to not only bless us, but others as well. This is the true heart of God and is the real heart of the prophetic.

RECOGNIZING TRUE THRONE ROOM PROPHETS

Now that we understand the various elements of Throne Room prophecy and how God will reveal things to you, let's take a look at the characteristics of a true, genuine Throne Room prophet. It's important to know how they differ from those who are not called to be prophets but perhaps prophesy from time to time.

So, what is the definition of a prophet? In the New Testament, *Thayer's Greek Definitions* describes the New Testament prophet as "one who solemnly declares what he has received by inspiration, especially concerning future events." Other words are often used to describe the prophet's function, including "to hear, sense, see, and to know by the anointing of the Holy Spirit; to instruct, comfort, empower, encourage, convict, discern, and foretell certain future events."

The word *prophet* in the Old Testament Hebrew is *nabiy*, which is simply a man inspired of God. A female is referred to as prophetess, which is *nebiyah*, or a woman inspired of God. Here is where prophets differ from those who simply prophesy. Any Christian can receive prophetic or divine inspiration, but a prophet is unique because his inspiration is often designed specifically for speaking to a wider audience and communicating a special message from God. This means they may hear more specific words and instructions at a higher level of authority and responsibility. The *Brown-Driver-Briggs Hebrew and English Lexicon* states that a prophet's express purpose is to be a spokesman or spokeswoman. How is he a spokesman?

He prophesies the things that God wants to say; this is a regular job requirement for the Throne Room prophet.

The Father has specifically chosen His spokespersons, the prophets, giving them a special grace to hear and speak for Him. They are to repeat the Lord's heart, mind, will, intent, and agenda through the means of prophecy. They are not better than those who are not called to such an office, but rather graced to see, hear, and perceive at a level that often forthtells, like John, the things the Lord is revealing that will come hereafter. This does not imply that the person who is not called to be a prophet will never be privy to knowing, seeing, or hearing specific events, but it will not typically be at a grace level that a Throne Room prophet has been given.

Just because we may evangelize like an evangelist or teach and love people like a pastor, it doesn't mean we are called to those offices. The offices of the evangelist and pastor carry a special grace level for what they do. As believers, we may do some of the things they do, but we are not all graced with the same level of revelation, anointing, or function as those who are called to these offices. It is the same way with prophets and those who may prophesy. Of course, all believers may be shown things by the Lord at times, just as prophets are shown things. This can come as a result of their personal prayer life or their disciplined walk with the Lord. However, the spiritual position, grace, authority, and responsibility given to a prophet is different than what is given to one who prophesies as a believer.

One important difference that separates a prophet from a person simply used in prophecy is that they are granted an office or a set position by Jesus, which is confirmed by church leadership. The prophet's office is given to some, not all (see 1 Cor. 12:28-29).

It's important to truly understand that for a person to function as a prophet they *must* be given a set position. Overlooking this element is often one of the reasons there is confusion over who is a prophet and who isn't. Titles can be tossed around, but this set position cannot be attained by someone giving themselves the title of "prophet." It must be established by church leadership. There are plenty of people all over the internet who claim to be prophets, but who appointed them? Who are they connected to, and who set them into such a position?

The fivefold ministry gifts given by Jesus in Ephesians 4:11 are there for the purpose of leading the Church as we see in verse 12, which says they are given for the "perfecting of the saints." In other words, their function is to bring the people of God to maturity. This speaks of positional authority. Yes, positional authority is granted by Jesus first and foremost, but then those to whom He gives those gifts must then be appointed and set into place by the elders or established leadership who have this authority.

We see this pattern throughout the New Testament when leaders were ordained into position. For example, you can have a gift of budgeting and have a great skill for handling finances, but this would not qualify you to carry the title or position of a bank president. In order to be the bank president, you would have to be recognized, received, and placed in that office. You couldn't just appoint yourself, go into any bank and let them know that since you have a gift for handling money, you should now carry the title of bank president. Neither can we do the same thing with any of the five spiritual offices of ministry. We cannot self-appoint or give ourselves a title and take over in an office that we haven't been positioned to carry, just because we have a gifting. Having a gift doesn't mean we have been granted a position of a higher authority or responsibility. This is why, as we have said, Jesus set some, not all, to be prophets in their office.

Acts 13 also shows us how prophets were set into positions and recognized within the local church.

> *Now there were in the church that was at Antioch certain prophets and teachers; as Barnabas, and Simeon that was called Niger, and Lucius of Cyrene, and Manaen, which had been brought up with Herod the tetrarch, and Saul* (Acts 13:1).

The prophets mentioned in this verse were connected to the local church, serving and functioning as prophets with the necessary character and fruit that qualified them to be titled as prophets. They were not spiritual mavericks or lone rangers; rather, their connection to the church helped to mark them as genuine prophets. This is clear in the example of the prophet Agabus, who came with other prophets from the Jerusalem church to Antioch. He prophesied a warning about a great famine that would take place globally.

> *Now in these days there came down prophets from
> Jerusalem unto Antioch. And there stood up one
> of them named Agabus, and signified by the Spirit
> that there should be a great famine over all the
> world: which came to pass in the days of Claudius*
> (Acts 11:27-28 ASV).

Such a prophetic word of warning was received in Antioch
because he obviously was recognized as a genuine prophet
connected to the Jerusalem church.

Why was his word of warning received? It was because of
his connection to the Jerusalem church. We see he had both a
spiritual and church connection, which gave him validity. In
would be safe to consider that he must have had a solid track
record of proven prophecies that those in the church of Antioch
knew. This helped his word to be discerned as being a genuine
word from the Lord. It is when there are words of direction,
correction, and warnings spoken that we must consider not just
the words prophesied or the prophet speaking, but their church
connection, spiritual covering, and track record. Agabus had all
of these—so not only was he received as a genuine prophet, but
his prophetic warning was received as well.

This is why when hearing prophetic words of warning
or prophetic words that have to do with global and national
events, it is necessary is to ask the questions, "Who are they,
what are they connected to, and are they recognized as being
genuine by true spiritual authority?" When these things are
established, their title and function will carry a greater impact
and authority, and they will be found trustworthy.

Those who stand in the prophetic office have an anointing and grace that consistently rests upon them to speak the word of the Lord regularly, not just on occasion. Their prophecies also go beyond exhortation, edification, and comfort, as they give more directive, forthtelling words. Their office carries an authority to prophesy on multiple platforms such as to individuals, local church, global church, and the nations. Here are a few examples from Scripture of some of the different expressions of the prophetic office:

- Prophets over nations: *"I have this day set thee over the nations"* (Jer. 1:10).
- Prophets to the Body of Christ: *"Exhorted the brethren"* (Acts 15:32).
- Prophets in local churches: *"at Antioch certain prophets and teachers"* (Acts 13:1).
- Prophets of events: prophet Agabus prophesied a famine (see Acts 11:27-28).
- Prophets to individuals: Agabus to Paul (see Acts 21:11).
- Singing prophets and intercession: David ministered prophetically in song and in prayer (see 1 Sam. 16).

PROPHETS AND PROPHECY STILL EXIST TODAY

The prophet's office and prophecy still exist today because the Lord is still speaking. Some have suggested that these two things have passed away and are no longer needed. The argument of some is that the Scripture says that prophecies will cease.

> *Charity never faileth: but whether there be prophecies, they shall fail; whether there be tongues, they shall cease; whether there be knowledge, it shall vanish away. For we know in part, and we prophesy in part. But when that which is perfect is come, then that which is in part shall be done away* (1 Corinthians 13:8-10).

This verse doesn't mean that prophecy has already ceased but rather that when we are in Heaven one day we won't need the gift of prophecy because everything will have been perfected. We can further conclude that if prophecy passed away then so has knowledge because that is mentioned in this same verse as prophecy. So, this verse is speaking of the perfect coming in regard to Heaven, when we will not only have Jesus who is *the* Prophet and His word for all eternity, but we will not need prophecy because we will know all things completely (see 1 Cor. 13:12).

The second verse often used to justify that prophecy and prophets have been done away with is Luke 16:16: *"The law and the prophets were until John: since that time the kingdom of God is preached, and every man presseth into it."* Some reading the King James Version think that the prophet's ministry has passed away, but the Amplified Bible, Classic Edition of this passage clearly states the messages of the prophets were pointing specifically to the period of time until John.

Until John came, there were the Law and the Prophets; since then the good news (the Gospel) of the kingdom of God is being preached, and everyone strives violently to go in [would force his own way rather than God's way into it].

However, it does not say the office, functions, and gifting of the prophet ended, but rather that the specific messages of the Old Testament prophets pointed to the Messiah. If the ministry of the prophet has become obsolete, then it makes what Jesus appointed and established in both Ephesians 4:11 and First Corinthians 12:28 obsolete. It also would disqualify the words of the prophet Agabus.

PROPHETS EDIFY AND CARRY AUTHORITY

Not only is God still speaking, but His prophets are prophesying His words today. They have been set and positioned to edify or build up the saints just as all of the fivefold ministry gifts do.

And he gave some, apostles; and some, prophets; and some, evangelists; and some, pastors and teachers; for the perfecting of the saints, for the work of the ministry, for the edifying of the body of Christ (Ephesians 4:11-12).

This verse also provides another way to help discern genuine prophets and prophecy. Notice it says, *"for the edifying of the body of Christ."* When a prophecy or someone prophesying is constantly speaking harshly or using words that sound judgmental, things get out of balance. Prophets are to build up and edify God's people and add their part in leading them into maturity and perfection. When this important element is not prioritized by the prophet, they will often start going the wrong direction and eventually become consistently false.

There are people who believe that in order to be considered a true prophet, that person must have a stern delivery and message. This is a misperception and has led to many prophecies that are overly expressive. Of course, prophets should carry authority, just as Jesus had authority on His words, but there is a vast difference between *having* authority and acting as if you do. Some of the most genuine prophets I know do not shout or express themselves in a harsh tone. They are just the opposite—soft-spoken and gentle. Now, some are more forthright in their manner and that can be fine, too, as long as their prophetic words are delivered in grace to edify the recipients.

There is no place for embarrassing or belittling anyone in the effort to appear powerful. Sure, prophetic words can carry warnings and admonitions—but when they do, caution must be exercised to ensure that what is communicated serves to lead the listener into faith, not fear, shame, or hopelessness. This is an important thing to remember if you desire to be used by God in prophecy. Make sure what you say, and *how* you say it, is building up and comforting the person or audience you are speaking to.

In saying this, let's touch on the prophet's authority and what it truly means to have authority on prophetic words. A prophet's authority often foretells the future at a deeper level of accuracy than the authority of those who are not called to this office. It's not so much in how they communicate but rather in the depth, detail, and precision of the message. Prophets are often shown future events that will occur in someone's life or on the earth and communicate them with marked accuracy. Now, a believer may at times have things shown to them regarding future events, but it will typically not be at the level of consistency or precision of the prophet.

The apostle John was able to see future events as shown him by the Lord. *"And I will shew thee things which must be hereafter"* (Rev. 4:1). The meaning of "things which must come hereafter" is a reference to future events. This is paramount in the prophet's ministry. Information about future events was going to be disclosed to the apostle John, and he received that information with precise accuracy. However, notice that it never mentions a specific date or time that these events would take place. I mention this point because some believe that if a prophet speaks of a future event to come, there should be a time frame involved. The fact of the matter is most of us want to hear time frames! We like to hear what year, month, or day something will happen, but this shouldn't be a requirement for prophets. This expectation can either cause prophets to misspeak, by causing them to try and give a date or time frame that God didn't give them, or can cause them to be misunderstood. This should serve as a reminder for us in the prophetic that if God doesn't speak a date, a year, or a specific time, then we should be cautious about declaring or inserting one. The prophet's focus should be on communicating future events with authority and accuracy and there should be depth and a notable anointing on their words.

I do want to mention that when it comes to accuracy, the prophets of the Bible were not always 100 percent accurate because human error is always involved. I will give some examples and discuss this in detail in Chapter Five. I'm not saying prophets can go around missing it all the time, and they most certainly should be accurate, but a prophet's authority cannot rest on accuracy alone. Accuracy must go hand in hand with the other elements of authority we have mentioned, including a notable anointing and a detailed depth of message.

When we look at Jesus, it wasn't so much the accuracy of His words that got people's attention, though that is important—it was the weight of what He communicated. This is what they said about Jesus regarding the authority upon His words:

> *And they were all amazed, insomuch that they questioned among themselves, saying, What thing is this? what new doctrine is this? for with authority commandeth he even the unclean spirits, and they do obey him* (Mark 1:27).

Like Jesus, true prophets speak with the weight of the Throne Room and of Him who is seated on that Throne. Something to consider when discerning whether a prophecy or prophet is accurate is that accuracy is often in the eye of the beholder. What do I mean? Just as they say beauty is in the eye of the beholder, so is prophecy. This means some people will be drawn to or believe that something is beautiful, while others may not think so and even find fault. Some will recognize a prophetic word as accurate, while others will not. This can be because so often people believe what they want to believe about a prophecy, either looking for any reason to discount the word or the prophet or because they misread and misunderstand the word. This is why, when accurately discerning a prophet and prophecy, there is more to consider than just accuracy alone. We must be careful before calling a prophet or prophecy false or erroneous until we have considered all the factors.

People can argue accuracy if they really want to, but you can't deny all the other elements that should be evident in a Throne Room prophet's life and ministry. They will be known for speaking authentic words, but in addition, you will be aware of what they carry and what you feel when they speak from the Throne Room. The attention will always be upon the testimony or testifying of Jesus and will carry the correct spirit of prophecy when they speak.

> *And I fell at his feet to worship him. And he said unto me, See thou do it not: I am thy fellowservant, and of thy brethren that have the testimony of Jesus: worship God: for the testimony of Jesus is the spirit of prophecy* (Revelation 19:10).

This means the prophecies given should convey the heart, mind, will, intent, and agenda of the Lord that honors Him and makes us want to come to Him.

How did Jesus get this authority on His words that marked Him as a man sent from the Throne Room and speaking from the Throne Room? He prayed, seeking God's face and developing His heart with the Father, which resulted in power. Jesus' private prayer life produced public demonstrations of power and authority.

In the same way, when we invest in our relationship with the Father, we will carry a strong heavenly authority and so will the Throne Room prophecies we speak! This is why John hears a voice like a trumpet. It signifies a sound that is heard and recognizable.

> *After this I looked, and, behold, a door was opened in heaven: and the first voice which I heard was as it were of a trumpet talking with me* (Revelation 4:1).

Prophets and Throne Room prophecy must carry this same heavenly sound as God's trumpets in the earth. The sound of their voices and words will be with authority, weight, and a recognizable backing from Heaven, in the same way the scribes and Pharisees recognized these things about Jesus. These characteristics help us identify genuine prophets who are set in position by the Lord of the Church.

DISCERNING PROPHECY

One of the best ways to position ourselves to function in true prophecy is to learn to listen, watch, and wait.

> *Blessed is the man that heareth me, watching daily at my gates, waiting at the posts of my doors* (Proverbs 8:34 ASV).

Our learning to receive the Lord's words starts with spending time just listening to the Lord and hearing what He has to say. It is in spending time with Him in fellowship, not necessarily entrenched in trying to hear a word, that He begins to speak and we learn to recognize His voice. We also need to learn to watch, as the previous verse stated, meaning we must make sure we are focusing on the right things and not being distracted. This helps us carry the Lord's word with greater clarity. Finally, we need to always remember to wait on the Lord for His perspective and words that He would desire to speak. When we learn to listen, watch, and wait, it will cause us to carry the anointing and utterance of His Spirit, just like those we read about in the Bible and throughout history. The secret of all the those in the Bible was their ability to hear God's voice and it is still what marks the Throne Room prophet.

When discerning how the Lord speaks prophetically, I see a great example in what I refer to as the "prophetic" threefold cord (see Eccles. 4:12). This is what the gift of prophecy is in its basic definition. It is like a threefold cord that should not be broken whenever we are ministering in the prophetic. It is made up of the three parts we mentioned earlier—exhortation, edification, and comfort. *"But he that prophesieth speaketh unto men to edification, and exhortation, and comfort"* (1 Cor. 14:3). Most prophecy when given through a believer is this threefold cord type of prophecy. This cord is the strength and foundation of the prophetic gifting.

The three conditions of the earth mentioned in Genesis 1:2 coincide with how edification, exhortation, and comfort are ministered through prophecy.

*The earth was without form, and void; and dark-
ness was upon the face* (Genesis 1:2).

Think about the condition of the earth as it's described
here compared with mankind today. So many people are often
without form, void, and living in darkness, in need of God's
intervention. This is why we need prophecy! People are often
lonely and empty and need to be edified or built up. Each one
of us has a need to be loved and comforted. We also know
that man without God is in spiritual darkness and needs words
of encouragement or exhortation. We must do what God did
when seeing the condition of the earth—He spoke. He said,
"Let there be light!" This is exactly what prophecy does—it
brings light and life to people's hearts.

Now, this doesn't always apply to the office of the prophet
as they don't *only* minister in prophecy of exhortation, edification, and comfort. Though the spirit in which they deliver
the message should always offer hope or God's redemptive
plan help, they do stand in a set authority or office, which at
times requires them to speak words of confrontation, conviction, judgment, rebuke, and direction. Keep in mind that
they prophesy from a delegated office to deal with things at a
higher, more specific level of function and responsibility than
one who exercises the gift of prophecy. As we said previously,
they should build and edify. This is especially true with the
New Testament prophet as they minister under a covenant
of grace because Jesus' death on the Cross has given us love,
mercy, and forgiveness. Obviously, the Old Testament prophets did not minister under this same grace because the Lord

had not yet come to redeem mankind and establish the covenant of His mercy and grace through His shed blood.

There are times that prophets may, like Jeremiah, need to root out and pull down strongholds. In such cases, their prophecies may carry warning, rebuke, or correction in order to build and plant, bringing something positive that exhorts, edifies, and comforts.

> *See, I have this day set thee over the nations and over the kingdoms, to root out, and to pull down, and to destroy, and to throw down, to build, and to plant* (Jeremiah 1:10).

Again, this is more manifested in the prophet's office and not so much in the simple gift of prophecy through the believer.

Another important aspect of prophecy to keep in mind is timing. As we are seeking to accurately discern prophecy, let's consider three different periods of time that can be addressed through prophetic words. Sometimes hearers can get confused because they don't understand the season the Lord is speaking to them about. Whenever we hear a prophecy, it isn't necessarily speaking of something yet to happen. Prophetic words may apply to any time in our lives—past, present, or future. The Lord may be confirming or encouraging us with something from our past; He may reveal something in our present, to assure us that He knows exactly where we are and what is happening; or He may give us insight into something that will come to pass in the future, in order to direct or prepare us.

I call these *confirming* (past) words, *now* (present) words, and *future* (future) words. *Confirming* words confirm something we already know or something from our past.

- The early church spoke many confirming words (see Acts 14:22).
- Jesus told Nathaniel the exact place He'd seen him sitting (see John 1:43-51).

Now words address our current situation—for example, Jesus with the woman at the well: *"he whom thou now hast is not thy husband"* (John 4:18).

Future words reveal something about our future.

- It can be something we already know, such as when Agabus spoke of a famine that would come (see Acts 11:28).
- Or it can be a "new word"—something that hasn't entered our minds until it is spoken, such as Jesus prophesying Peter's death (see John 21:19).

Each type of prophetic word should come to fill the voids of life that people experience and should carry the heart of the Father for both individuals and larger groups. Don't forget, the goal of all prophecy is to reveal the heart of Him who sits on the Throne and to move people from where they are, further into the purposes of God.

Finally, there are true, wrong, and false prophecies. True prophecies are from the Lord and we will see the fruit of the prophetic word come to pass. Wrong words are those where part or all of the prophecy is wrong. This doesn't make the vessel or prophet false, as they may have simply misspoken. Perhaps all of the word was wrong, not being from the Lord, or part of the word was wrong—meaning they spoke out of their own heart, but not with purposeful intent to deceive or manipulate through devious means. When someone has a normal, trusted track record and the majority of their words are true, but they perhaps speak something wrong, that prophetic vessel or prophet should not immediately be disregarded. It is when *most* of their words are wrong that this can create confusion. It could be that the person prophesying needs to be held to a higher standard or, in some cases, they should be disregarded altogether. However, this should not be the case over a small number of honest mistakes. Remember, prophets grow in grace too, just like pastors, teachers, and just like we all do.

Obviously, false prophets and prophecies are meant to deceive, lead one in error, or draw attention to the one speaking. Scripture clearly warns us about those who speak prophetically with wicked intentions.

> *Beware of false prophets, which come to you in sheep's clothing, but inwardly they are ravening wolves* (Matthew 7:15).

> *And many false prophets shall rise, and shall deceive many* (Matthew 24:11).

If we remain close to the Lord and can hear His heart, we will be able to recognize true, wrong, and false prophecies.

Then we can keep ourselves and others from the damage the enemy brings by distorting the true prophetic.

Throughout this chapter, we've looked in detail at the ministry of the prophet and the functions of prophecy. Remember, first and foremost as prophets and prophetic people, we must stay in a place of humility where we allow the Lord to shape us. From that place, when we see the spiritual condition of man, we can truly release His prophetic words in the earth. God's heart is that *all* would know and walk with Him, and we have a great privilege as prophets, and believers who prophesy, to speak His words and convey His heart to people. As we allow the Lord to mold and shape us, we will become vessels who can bring great light to the darkness and lift up the hearts of men. I encourage you to get into that place with God in His presence—the Throne Room. Let Him make you everything He has called you to be and prophesy His words!

Chapter Four

PROPHECY AND DISCERNING THE SOURCE: FIRST, SECOND, OR THIRD HEAVEN?

> *"And immediately I was in the spirit: and, behold, a throne was set in heaven, and one sat on the throne."*
> —REVELATION 4:2

You may remember the year 1999, when countless people were in fear of a coming apocalyptic event that would hit the planet, stopping computers and anything that didn't have upgraded software to handle the new millennium we were entering. That event would be known as the Y2K computer

bug crisis. Everything that had to do with a computer, a chip, or non-updated software was expected to fail. It was thought that the crisis would cause planes to quit working and some feared they would fall out of the sky. The stock market was supposed to crash worldwide due to computer systems not being upgraded. People everywhere were in panic and fear as they were encouraged to prepare for major food shortages, chaos, and global crisis. Some believed that the government would have to get involved to establish order. As news outlets warned people of the impending doom, some prophets were even prophesying in agreement with the reports coming from the media. Whole churches were warning their congregations to be ready and encouraging them to store up food supplies. At the stroke of midnight, many things were expected to shut down.

I will never forget the experience I had the summer before this event was expected to happen. The Lord spoke to me that Y2K would not be as they were prophesying, discussing, and prognosticating. He said that the demonic forces from hell were trying to cross the new millennium ahead of His Church through the spirit of fear and that the agreement from those in the earth with this fear would cause our nation to be vulnerable to attacks. God wanted there to be faith, excitement, and expectation of His goodness and upcoming prophetic plan. This would be extended to a new generation that was arising in this new millennium. However, fear was trying to dominate and hinder what the Lord was desiring.

So much was being reported from the media and discussed by people in the earth, which I refer to as the first realm. If that wasn't enough, the very source or spirit you could feel affecting people was fear, panic, and worry—coming from the *second* realm. This place, also called the second heaven, is where the devil and his spiritual forces operate. The second heaven is the place we refer to as the atmosphere or space, and the Bible calls this "the heavenlies" (see Eph. 6:12 DARBY). This is why the devil is referred to as the prince of the power of the air (see Eph. 2:2). This is not Heaven as we would think of Heaven. The Bible refers to that as the *third* realm or what Paul the apostle referred to as the "third heaven," where he was caught up. So, we have the earth realm and its atmosphere, which is the first heaven; the second realm or heaven, which is space or the heavenlies; and the third heaven or the third realm, where God's Throne is.

In reference to this Y2K event, the enemy understood the power of agreement and caused not only the Lord's Church but those in the secular world to get into agreement with this spirit of fear. Fear is a spirit as recorded by the apostle Paul to his spiritual son Timothy (see 2 Tim. 1:7). Now, I am not implying one shouldn't be wise and prudent and heed sound warnings. However, I am drawing attention to the fact that often when warnings are made known, people can respond in fear, especially if such warnings become heightened or exaggerated because of people's wrong assumptions and misinformation. The is where the enemy and the spirit of fear get involved. As prophets and prophetic people, we must be able to discern the spirit behind such warnings as well as what God is saying from the third heaven.

There was tremendous fear surrounding the Y2K situation and people were falling into agreement with that spirit of fear. Yet I remember the Lord telling me Y2K would not be a big deal or as they said. Now this was opposite of what was being said at the time. Yet it was exactly as the Lord prophesied, as this global catastrophic event never happened as they had predicted.

In fact, the very night that the planes were supposed to fall from the sky. I took a flight overnight to go to a football game that would be potentially affected by the Y2K crisis, due to the flight times having me in the air at midnight. It was the best flight time and cheap price for a great football game matchup. I knew what the Lord said, even though it honestly messed with my head at times, but I was settled in my heart with what I'd heard from the Throne Room.

I and one other person were the only ones on the flight that night. We had all the snacks to ourselves! It was also a great opportunity to share with the flight crew what the Lord said and to reassure some of them that it was going to be alright. The earth was not going to crash, and neither would the plane. The sad thing is, I believe the very spirit of fear and the agreement people had with it, which had come from the first and second heavens (the earth and its atmosphere), opened a place of vulnerability. I believe that mass fear opened the door to the spirit of terrorism that would soon follow as we saw just a little less than two years later on September 11th, 2001.

The reason I say all this is because we need to understand that in accurately discerning prophecy and the prophetic interpretation surrounding certain events, we must know which realm we are listening to and how it is affecting the current situation and what is being communicated. This is especially true concerning the various avenues of communication. Whether it's from prophets or the media speaking to whatever the latest fears are, it is important to understand which realm that information is coming from and the source of their words, perspectives, and insights. This is especially true regarding prophets. Now obviously, we can't expect the secular media to get their perspective from God, but sometimes prophets listen to these media outlets and their messages get tainted by the news reports. We must ask ourselves, is this coming from the first heaven, the second heaven, or the third heaven? Then we can determine how those who hear are being influenced.

Genuine prophets must not be caught up in or influenced by things in the earth. This is especially true with what is on the news, and they certainly must not repeat the words and agenda of the enemy coming from the earth or the second heaven. If they do, they will then speak wrongly or even give false prophecies. The second heaven is the location of demons, spiritual warfare, and witchcraft, which all desire for us to give them access to the earth realm where they can steal, kill, destroy, and deceive.

We must never forget the power of our agreement and how both God and the enemy work by what we add our agreement to. This is why God has prophets who speak from the Throne Room, the third heaven—so we may believe *those* words and add our agreement. This gives the Spirit of God access and freedom to carry those words and bring changes in people's lives and on the earth.

The enemy, the devil, also has his prophets or those who "prophesy," meaning they repeat and agree with his agenda, lies, and deceptions. This not only affects individuals but will also affect spiritual climates in the heavenlies and, therefore, events on the earth. The Bible shows us how the enemy uses the first and second realms to release wrong and false information through the means of prophecy. As in the examples of the prophets that King Ahab sought, they not only told him what he wanted to hear, but they gave misleading prophecies. There were false prophets of Baal who ministered under a false, occultic spirit driven by the hands of Jezebel, King Ahab's wife. It is not hard to discern what sources they were prophesying from, which caused them to speak false words. Their prophecies were not from Heaven but were rather influenced by evil spirits operating in both the heavenlies and on the earth. Their words were also what the king wanted them to say, which resulted in a release of hell's agenda. This not only affected the king but also the whole nation of Israel.

If we spend time dwelling in fear, anxiety, or popular trends, news topics, and discussions, our perspectives will become skewed and may keep us from discerning which realm is influencing our lives the most. It is so vital that we have Heaven's words more than ever right now, so we can pierce through the darkness, deception, fears, and confusion that exist today. It takes vessels in the earth who will live and walk in the light in the midst of darkness and who will seek out the truth from the Throne Room itself.

I WAS IN THE SPIRIT

When the apostle John was called to come up higher by the Lord, we find the source of his prophetic perspective and instruction. The Scripture tells us in verse 2 of Revelation 4 that immediately John was in the spirit.

> *And immediately I was in the spirit: and, behold, a throne was set in heaven, and one sat on the throne* (Revelation 4:2).

While in the spirit, he received prophetic words from the third heaven that he was ordered to declare. Notice, he had to be in the spirit in order to correctly perceive the word of the Lord and even how he was encountering the Lord through heavenly experiences.

In the same way, genuine prophets must perceive by the Holy Spirit and through their spirit so their prophetic words do not come from their own minds and emotions. Now, at the same time, we will also see that the information we receive, even if from the Throne Room, still gets filtered through our minds, wills, and emotions. This is why it's so important to walk and operate in the spirit so there can be pure flow of prophetic revelation and giftings in our lives.

So, just what does this verse mean by being "in the spirit"? It is where your spiritual senses transcend or exceed your natural five senses and your awareness of the spirit realm becomes greater than what you are experiencing in the natural realm. We will discuss the different realms from which revelation, information, and spiritual activity come in this chapter. As we can see in this moment with John, it is a spiritual state or place that allowed him to see, hear, feel, and experience with his spiritual senses what was taking place in the third heaven. We must remember that we live in a physical earth suit, which is our body; we possess a soul, which is our mind, will, and emotions; but our spirit is who we *really* are.

Because John was in the spirit, he could accurately receive genuine prophetic revelation to share with others. This is vital because it was when he was in the spirit that he began to hear the words of Heaven and see things from Heaven's perspective. His revelation was clearly coming from the Throne Room, or the third heaven.

Being in the spirit and operating from this heavenly place is what will take you higher in your gifting, sensitivity, and preciseness as it did with the apostle John. When words spoken with "thus saith the Lord" often do not happen, it is because the one speaking either wasn't sharing it from a Throne Room experience or they weren't in the spirit when they spoke it. Sometimes people will speak from their own mind, experience, feelings, or even personal biases. When prophets and prophetic vessels are not speaking by the anointing of the Holy Spirit but through their human spirit, it will cause the words they carry to not have Heaven's backing. As a result, their prophecies don't come to pass or what they say lacks heavenly weight and authority.

Remember, Jesus walked in the spirit, and people often were amazed by the authority they saw in Him (see Matt. 7:28-29; Mark 1:22). The pure flow of the Holy Spirit's anointing manifested through Him in power. How did He maintain a life in the Spirit and create this heavenly flow? Jesus spent countless hours in the Spirit and in prayer with His Father and therefore knew His Father's words. These words were already rich inside Jesus before He ever ministered or spoke publicly. It is the key for us as well—to spend time with the Lord in the Spirit through prayer, reading God's Word, praying in the Spirit, and living spiritual lives. We are then positioned to speak for our heavenly Father, who is Spirit, because our words have come from heart-to-heart, spirit-to-spirit conversations with the Lord. This is how we not only become more sensitive to the spirit realm but also walk in the Spirit.

Walking in the Spirit is a continual practicing of the presence of the Lord throughout your day. It is practiced in your speech, your conduct, and by staying aware of His presence and in constant communication with Him. This helps to position you to recognize when prophetic revelation is coming from the Holy Spirit and what He is wanting to reveal to you or speak through you. When one chooses to be in the Spirit, or as the Scripture says, to live and walk in the Spirit, there will be evident fruit. *"This I say then, Walk in the Spirit, and ye shall not fulfil the lust of the flesh"* (Gal. 5:16). We must walk in the Spirit and not in the flesh, meaning the way of sin, and not compromise or participate in what the Scripture declares are the works of flesh.

> *Now the doings (practices) of the flesh are clear*
> *(obvious): they are immorality, impurity, indecency,*
> *idolatry, sorcery, enmity, strife, jealousy, anger (ill*

temper), selfishness, divisions (dissensions), party spirit (factions, sects with peculiar opinions, heresies), envy, drunkenness, carousing, and the like (Galatians 5:19-21 AMPC).

When we choose to live and walk in the Spirit, others will then see the evidence (or fruit) of our walk and what the Bible calls the fruit of the Spirit. *"But the fruit of the Spirit is love, joy, peace, longsuffering, gentleness, goodness, faith"* (Gal. 5:22). When you walk in the Spirit, you will naturally manifest the fruit of the Spirit. It will enhance your gifting and also will be visible in the prophecies you speak. A pure spirit and life will produce pure prophecy, even though it gets filtered through our own human soul. If our soul is filled with works of the flesh by the carnal things we choose to look at, hear, and even do, then it will taint the pure stream of God's revelation from His Spirit to our spirit. Our revelation is then hindered by our flesh and compromised soul. I am certainly not saying everyone has to be a perfect vessel but, rather, *pure* vessels who want to live a life in the Spirit. As we are intentional about purity, it will cause us to be in the Spirit more and better positioned to be entrusted with what is on the Lord's heart.

Now as we said, if one chooses to not walk in the Spirit, but rather chooses to live a life in the flesh and of compromise, it will hinder them. The spirit behind their words and revelations will be tainted and affected by their fleshly tastes, decisions, and lifestyles. Once we choose the life of the Spirit, we will be hungry for more of what the Spirit of God wants to do and say. It will be like a magnet that draws His words, His thoughts, and His glory to us. When we open our mouths to speak His words, even though we are human vessels, we will have a pure, Holy-Spirit-inspired prophetic message.

One key to being in the spirit like the apostle John was, as he was caught up into this heavenly experience, comes by praying in the Spirit. This will aid us in in receiving prophetic revelation from the Lord and help sharpen our prophetic gifting. Praying in the Spirit takes our spiritual office as a prophet or our giftings and life to another level. Our hearing, receiving, and ability to prophesy all increase in accuracy.

We can further understand this powerful connection between prophesying and praying in the Spirit by looking at the Day of Pentecost. Consider for a moment what happened when the believers were baptized in the Holy Spirit and began to speak in tongues. The Bible says they magnified God, which began to open a flow of power and boldness. This is evident in Peter as he stood up and preached a prophetic sermon in Acts 2. He declared that what he and the 120 had received was a fulfilment of the prophet Joel's prophecy, that sons and daughters would prophesy and have visions and that dreams would be given to the young and old. In other words, what the group in the upper room had received was an inflow of supernatural power so they could operate in the prophetic!

We continue to find this powerful connection of prophecy and speaking in tongues when the apostle Paul came to Ephesus and ministered to a group of twelve disciples. When he prayed for them, Scripture tells us they didn't just speak in in tongues, but they also prophesied!

And when Paul had laid his hands upon them, the Holy Ghost came on them; and they spake with tongues, and prophesied (Acts 19:6).

Think for a moment of the pure stream and flow from Heaven that came *to* them and now *through* them. They were not only filled with His Spirit but prophesying by His inspiration and divine ability. The same is true for us!

I have learned firsthand how the increase of prophetic revelation, insight, and a deeper level to the prophetic giftings become sharper and more frequent by a committed life and by praying in the Spirit. The more I pray in tongues, the more sensitive my spirit becomes to the Lord. I experience an increase of God's thoughts, impressions, and voice. If you are filled with the Holy Spirit and speak in tongues, I challenge you to increase your praying in the Spirit and watch the prophetic flow that increases within you. You will receive more precise prophetic insights from the Throne Room, the third heaven! It is one very vital way that you are "in the Spirit" like the apostle John. Being in the Spirit comes by praying in the Spirit, walking in the Spirit, and living in the Spirit (see Gal. 5:25)!

BE FILLED WITH THE SPIRIT!

Now, if you haven't yet been filled with the Holy Spirit with the evidence of speaking in tongues, I want to share with you how to receive that. The first requirement is that you are saved, by inviting Jesus to come into your heart and forgive your sins.

This begins your life and walk in the Spirit. This is the water of salvation Jesus offered the woman at the well in John 4, which springs up unto everlasting life.

> *But whosoever drinketh of the water that I shall give him shall never thirst; but the water that I shall give him shall be in him a well of water springing up into everlasting life* (John 4:14).

However, there is a separate experience in addition to the new birth—the baptism of the Holy Spirit, which helps us to live a life in the Spirit. Jesus talked about this wonderful experience by likening it to a river of living water or living power gushing out of us!

> *In the last day, that great day of the feast, Jesus stood and cried, saying, If any man thirst, let him come unto me, and drink. He that believeth on me, as the scripture hath said, out of his belly shall flow rivers of living water. (But this spake he of the Spirit, which they that believe on him should receive: for the Holy Ghost was not yet given; because that Jesus was not yet glorified)* (John 7:37-39).

If you have received the Lord as your personal Savior but have not been yet filled with His Spirit and prayed in tongues, you can receive that today in the same way you received salvation by asking Jesus to come into your heart. You received that *simply by believing you received.* Do the same by asking the Holy Spirit to fill you. Then begin opening your mouth and speak out the heavenly words He is giving you. Many people begin to hear syllables or sounds down inside them; the key is just open your mouth and begin to speak. The Holy Spirit gives the utterances. In other words, He takes those sounds you make and gives them meaning. It's a spiritual language—not your own dialect but a supernatural one. Again, your job is to just speak out or repeat what He is giving you. It's not in your head, even though you will process it in your mind, but rather it's from your belly, meaning your heart or the innermost part of you. This is the beginning of a lifelong journey that will help you be in the spirit like John. It is also a reminder to us who are already filled with the Holy Spirit to increase our praying in the Spirit. As we do, we will see an increase in the kind of prophetic that causes us to come up higher in the things of the Lord.

Regular praying in tongues connects you to the heart of the Father as the Scripture tells us that he who speaks in an unknown tongue speaks mysteries to God (see 1 Cor. 14:2). Praying in the Spirit helps position us to walk in the Spirit and to have a tangible presence of God upon our lives and words that we speak. Not only will we speak mysteries to God, but His mysteries or secrets will be revealed to us and through us in prophecy and the gifts of the Spirit. When we pray in tongues on a regular basis, we will not only have the right prophetic perspectives, but what we prophesy will be more accurate. In addition, it will help us to prophesy not by our own perspective of our mind, will, or emotions; rather, it will be from God's Spirit to our spirit, filtered correctly through our soul.

FILTERS OF THE HUMAN SOUL

The human soul is involved with any person prophesying or operating in the gifts of the Spirit. This is a point where prophecy or prophetic ministers can miss it. Sometimes the source from which they are receiving and speaking may not be the Spirit of God but rather their own human soul. Another reason is they could be ministering out of what they heard from people, what they heard on the news, or what is influencing them in the first and second heaven. When this happens, prophetic revelation is hindered because their soul is affected by what they hear with their natural ears and continually dwell upon.

We must be reminded that there is a right and purposeful place for our mind, will, and emotions when it comes to prophecy. The truth of the matter is every prophecy, vision, and dream or gift of the Spirit gets filtered through our soul. This means our mind, will, and emotions are involved in every prophecy we give, no matter who we are or how long we have walked in prophetic things. The more we connect to the Lord in the Spirit and seek to walk, live, and pray in the Spirit, the less we hinder the flow of His heart and words. The result is that the words we speak will be more effective as they are filtered through our souls.

True prophecy's source is always the Holy Spirit, as He reveals things to our spirits, even though the revelation is subject to our human souls. This is why we must fine-tune our spiritual hearing. Remember, Jesus said, "Let those who have ears to hear, hear what the Spirit is saying" (see Rev. 3:6). It is far too easy to formulate our own opinions and perspectives from what we spend time listening to and thinking about. Again, when we spend time in His Word, prayer, and praying in the Spirit, we will carry the third-heaven perspective. This helps keep us sharp in the prophetic, even though we may experience spiritual opposition and interference from the first and second heavens.

We must remember the Lord is perfect and so are His words. However, this doesn't mean the one prophesying or all prophecy spoken is going to be perfect. It also doesn't mean that it won't be affected by our soul or influenced by the first and second heaven. Revelation given by God is perfect, but it is always subject to the imperfections of the human soul. Now, in the case of those who penned the Scriptures, the perfect Word of God being spoken was uniquely and sovereignly overshadowed and protected by the Holy Spirit.

> *Above all, you must understand that no prophecy of Scripture came about by the prophet's own interpretation of things. For prophecy never had its origin in the human will, but prophets, though human, spoke from God as they were carried along by the Holy Spirit* (2 Peter 1:20-21 NIV).

Even then, you will still find God using the writers' personalities and emotions to speak forth His words! The prophecy of Scripture had to have the special protection of the Lord because it is the final authority and measuring stick for all prophets, gifts, and prophecies. This is why the Bible, when speaking in context about prophets and prophecy, tells us to test all things. The way we do that is to hold everything up against the Scripture.

> *Do not spurn the gifts and utterances of the prophets [do not depreciate prophetic revelations nor despise inspired instruction or exhortation or warning]. But test and prove all things [until you can recognize] what is good; [to that] hold fast* (1 Thessalonians 5:20-21 AMPC).

In the case of a prophet who prophesies today, he may hear the word exactly as the Spirit of God is saying it but can also put his own interpretation upon it when speaking it or even after it is spoken. That's why Paul says we see in a mirror dimly (see 1 Cor. 13:12). We don't know everything; our souls are always involved in giving and receiving prophetic words. This is why Paul taught us that *"we know in part, and we prophesy in part"* (1 Cor. 13:9).

When we realize that every prophetic word spoken is filtered through the human soul, we can better discern prophecies we receive and hear. It also helps us understand why a true prophet or someone with a genuine desire to prophesy accurately might miss it on occasion. This person was likely not trying to be false, manipulative, or deceptive. They intended to speak the word of the Lord, but their own soul interfered. This doesn't make them or their prophetic word false—it is simply wrong.

Have you ever had a dream that was so real, but one part of the dream made no sense or made you feel like you'd had a pizza dream? The dream came to pass even though you never figured out that one strange part. This happened because, although it was a true dream from the Spirit of God to your spirit, your soul was still involved. Your human mind can continue to dream about other things even after dreaming something that genuinely came from the Lord.

This is also what happens sometimes when a prophetic word is spoken and 99 percent of it is spot on, with a small word or point that doesn't seem to line up. Again, the human factor was involved in what was spoken. Let me give you an example from Scripture. As we look at Samuel, we'll see where his own human filter was involved. Many people use Samuel as an example for why people or prophets should never make a mistake when they prophesy. They base this on First Samuel 3:19, which says Samuel's words never fell to the ground. We will discuss in detail why the Bible says this about Samuel in the next chapter; however, we do find that Samuel's own soul was involved in his prophetic revelation at the house of Jesse.

> *The Lord said to Samuel, "How long will you mourn for Saul, since I have rejected him as king over Israel? Fill your horn with oil and be on your way; I am sending you to Jesse of Bethlehem. I have chosen one of his sons to be king"* (1 Samuel 16:1 NIV).

First, notice that Samuel was still in mourning over Saul. His own emotions were obviously affecting him enough that the Lord corrected him. So it's possible that even as he went to the house of Jesse, his own personal experiences were having an effect on him. Samuel obeyed God and went to the house of Jesse to anoint the next king of Israel. However, he initially chose the wrong person when he assumed Eliab was the Lord's chosen. The human filter of his soul was involved and the Lord had to remind him not to look on the outward appearance.

> *When they arrived, Samuel saw Eliab and thought, "Surely the Lord's anointed stands here before the Lord." But the Lord said to Samuel, "Do not consider his appearance or his height, for I have rejected him. The Lord does not look at the things people look at. People look at the outward appearance, but the Lord looks at the heart"* (1 Samuel 16:6-7 NIV).

Even after this, Samuel had to continue working through the filtering of his soul several more times as each of Jesse's sons was brought before him. Now he began to accurately discern the word of the Lord and to perceive correctly from his spirit. Once he was able to do that, it enabled him to prophesy correctly. As each of Jesse's sons were brought, Samuel knew none of them were the one the Lord had chosen. However, he still didn't have a clear word on who was chosen. Finally, he asked if there was another, and it wasn't until David was brought that he knew who the Lord's anointed was. He was no longer being moved by his own human filter but now by his spirit.

> *Then Jesse called Abinadab and had him pass in front of Samuel. But Samuel said, "The Lord has not chosen this one either." Jesse then had Shammah pass by, but Samuel said, "Nor has the Lord chosen this one." Jesse had seven of his sons pass before*

Samuel, but Samuel said to him, "The Lord has not chosen these." So he asked Jesse, "Are these all the sons you have?" "There is still the youngest," Jesse answered. "He is tending the sheep." Samuel said, "Send for him; we will not sit down until he arrives" (1 Samuel 16:8-11 NIV).

We can conclude from this that even though Samuel did eventually discern the one the Lord had anointed, it did not happen without his soul being involved in the prophetic revelation.

Another example is when Ezekiel had to eat a heavenly scroll. He put it in his mouth and then it reached his belly. Through this spiritual encounter, Ezekiel shows us this process of how a prophetic word given by the Lord is filtered through our soul before it reaches our spirit. It further reveals the source of information, or the realm where he received this word. It had come from the Throne Room, the third heaven.

And he said to me, "Son of man, eat what is before you, eat this scroll; then go and speak to the people of Israel." So I opened my mouth, and he gave me the scroll to eat. Then he said to me, "Son of man, eat this scroll I am giving you and fill your stomach with it." So I ate it, and it tasted as sweet as honey in my mouth. He then said to me: "Son of man, go now to the people of Israel and speak my words to them" (Ezekiel 3:1-4 NIV).

Prophetic words and revelations always pass through the human filters of our soul as we see with Ezekiel. He was instructed to first eat the scroll handed to him from Heaven before he would prophesy. In other words, the scroll represents the prophetic revelation God is bringing to us that we must chew on or process before we are quick to share it or speak. This is especially important for prophets.

Ezekiel had to take time to digest or process the word of the Lord, which is what the scroll represents. Him "eating it" or it entering through his mouth speaks of a process. It points to the fact that he had to see it, receive it, and digest it, all of which must include the soul or mind. Again, it was filtered through his mind, will, and emotions before it would be deposited into his belly or spirit. Once it was processed through his soul and had become sure in his spirit, he could then speak this prophetic word accurately. Notice Ezekiel 3:2 says it had to become "sweet as honey." This tells us he had to process it through his soul so he could minister the word in the right spirit or with the right taste and grace! Ezekiel's encounter shows us how important it is for the word of the Lord to get into your belly and spirit after it is filtered through your human soul. Often when a prophetic word is given by the Lord, it is easy for our heads to get in the way. However, our human reasoning must not interfere or hinder the word of the Lord from being deposited and ministered from our spirit. This is often why it is a process.

Remember, the Bible says the things of the Spirit are foolish for those who try to figure them out in their head or judge them only with their mind (see 1 Cor. 2:14). This can also be why prophecy and genuine prophets are misunderstood or labeled falsely—some hearers will hear them from a place of soulish understanding rather than through spiritual discernment and understanding. Additionally, those offering their opinions and judgments are sometimes doing so not from their spirits but rather their souls or flesh. Spiritual things do require common sense and biblical backing, but we must always seek to understand with our spirits.

It is important that we subject our souls to spiritual things and are wise about what we allow into our minds, wills, and emotions through what we see, hear, and feel. When we do so, we will find prophetic revelations pure and accurate as they enter our spirits. As a result, our words will carry more accuracy, authority, clarity, and purity.

Knowing this will help us to better discern whether a genuine prophet or prophetic word was from the Lord or not. We can better understand such questions as, "Did they speak it from their spirit? If so, how much was tainted or affected by their own mind, will, and emotions?"

For example, sometimes when we hear a prophecy that sounds right, the word doesn't come to pass, or it doesn't register with us in our spirits. Why is this? It is often because the prophetic word had too much of the person's own mind involved when they spoke it, meaning much of their own will and emotion was added to it. Another reason the word didn't seem accurate when it was spoken could be because the one judging the true prophecy put their own interpretation on the word and believed it to say something it didn't. The prophecy could be accurate, but their own mind interfered, causing them to see it as wrong or false. Their own human filters were involved in the hearing of the word and they did not discern it from their spirit. Like Samuel initially at the house of Jesse, people are sometimes moved by what they see, hear, and feel. This causes them to discern or judge from their own soul or perceptions rather than their spirits. This is often where we find ourselves agreeing with certain parts of a prophetic word and not others or discounting a word because we didn't like the way the prophet looked or how they ministered the word. As much as we don't like to admit it, we let outward appearances affect us.

My wife Brenda and I had this happen to us once with a prophet who ministered to us early in our marriage. He was dressed differently from how we normally expected a preacher to dress. Actually, it wasn't to our preference and his style and delivery were unusual as well. We initially began to dismiss him based on our own perceptions. What he prophesied was spot on; however, there was one part we didn't feel was accurate and that was when he said that we were called to pastor a church. You see, at the time we were traveling in the ministry and felt no calling to pastor. We didn't fully receive this word because of some hang-ups in our human souls, and at the time we didn't discern it in the spirit. Thank God we discovered that word was, in fact, right and so was that prophet—even though he didn't measure up to our expectations for dress, ministry style, and delivery. We have been pastoring for over twenty years today and love it. You see, we liked or agreed with certain parts of the prophecy, but other parts we didn't receive, simply based on our own interpretation and preferences.

This is where many prophets and prophecies are unfortunately mistreated, falsely accused, or wrongfully judged. We do what Samuel did with the human filter of his soul—we look on the outward appearance or discern things based on our biases, opinions, or hearsay and not from our spirits. So rather than be quick to mislabel the prophet or prophecy, we need to pause and ensure that there isn't something in us that needs to be adjusted. And remember, there isn't any rush to draw conclusions. Sometimes it's wise just put the word on the shelf, so to speak, and let it play out.

It is vital that we understand that if a word is spoken and it doesn't appear to initially come to pass, this does not necessarily make the vessel false or the word false, particularly when there was no purposeful manipulation, trickery, or deceit. Again, no one is without the filter of their soul when it comes to being a prophet or prophesying. This is why in the New Testament, the prophet and vessel are under grace, meaning there is room for human error, and truthfully, error is to be expected sometimes. Now, that is not saying that we just say anything we want and expect to get a pass. It just means there is space for people to make mistakes, even in the prophetic. And by keeping our souls (minds, wills, and emotions) pure, it will aid in allowing the prophetic words we are receiving from the Lord to be processed correctly and accurately.

We have to remember, when we hear a prophecy that is as if the Lord is speaking, that all humans have a soul and every prophetic revelation flows through this filter. Knowing this will help us as we learn to yield to the Holy Spirit and seek to minister to others. This will also help us when we listen to a prophecy—to discern correctly and not fall into unnecessary judgments and criticisms.

It is far too easy, when a hearing a prophetic word, to be quick to deem something or someone as false based on our own emotions rather than discerning correctly in the Spirit.

Even a genuine Throne Room prophet who speaks by and from the Spirit still processes the prophetic flow they are receiving through their own human soul. It is a reminder that we must all strive to have our words and giftings flow from the source and person of the Holy Spirit, through *our* spirits, and be delivered accurately without our souls being too involved.

We can always count on the fact that the Holy Spirit of God will show us and help us to discern what is of Him and what is not. That is why there can be wrong, false, wishful, and true prophecy—because of the vessels involved. God understands this, but still chooses to use human vessels who are a work in progress and who are progressing. Yet it should be our goal to go higher and to have excellence in all facets of our gifting, function, and how we are ministering in our spiritual gifts. This is the Lord's desire for us as well. Again, this comes by being reminded of the awesomeness of the One seated on the Throne and the distinct honor to represent Him and speak for Him. When we do, our gifting will go to another level, especially in the accuracy and manifestation of our gifts. The key is to speak by the Spirit of God and in the spirit and not of our own mind or things that we wish for and formulate them into prophetic words.

Because God has made each one of us unique, it is important to be who you are. However, when you are ministering a prophetic word, try not to have mannerisms or strange behaviors that draw the attention to you and away from the Lord and the word you have been given. People notice our ethics, mannerisms, and how we represent ourselves and our giftings. We understand uniqueness and diversity of expression in how we minister, but it is always wise to be genuine and to act normally, without coming across as strange or flakey. When we maintain our uniqueness without adding excessive expressions, people are better able to receive us and our words.

We can see the importance of accurately discerning the word of the Lord, understanding the human filter of the soul, and knowing what realm the information is coming from. Remember, we live in the information age. The perspectives we form through our minds, wills, and emotions can be affected by so many things. There is a source of every piece of information we are affected by. It comes from either the third heaven, the second heaven, or the earth realm (first heaven).

THE FIRST, SECOND, AND THIRD HEAVEN

Let's look at these three realms of information and how they affect things in the earth as well as what affects prophetic revelation. First is the Throne Room level, which is the third heaven or realm, where God is seated on His Throne and rules over all things. The second realm, we learned, is the spirit realm or the heavenlies, meaning the atmosphere—where the Scripture references satan as the prince of the power of the air. This realm is where much spiritual warfare is happening in the high places and is the source of divination, witchcraft, and the psychic realm. Then last, we know that information comes from the first heaven, including media and things that are spoken in and from the earth realm.

So how does one accurately discern prophetic words or what is coming from the different realms that we have been discussing? First and foremost, discernment comes as we make a habit and commitment to spend time with the Lord in the Spirit. In addition, it is protecting or possessing the human filter of our souls from dwelling on things that will affect us negatively or interfere with a pure life in the Spirit. Jesus even mentioned the importance of possessing our souls, meaning that like a horse, we put a bridle on it. *"In your patience possess ye your souls"* (Luke 21:19). This keeps our minds, wills, and emotions in check and keeps us sharp when it comes to discerning information from the three realms.

This is why spending time with the Lord, worshiping Him who is seated on the Throne, and living a life in the Spirit will help to discern the realm and the source from which things are being predicted or prophesied. You will be able to do so because your spiritual senses will be sharpened. You will discern God's character in a prophetic word, the spirit (or Spirit) behind it, because you have been with Him. As we mentioned, He is the source and the One from whom all true Throne Room prophecy comes.

Yet to accurately discern what realm is speaking, it is important to not get caught up with the fears, the trends, or the cultural mindsets in the earth realm, or what we call the first realm. We can lose our discernment, hindering our spiritual sensitivity to God's Spirit and Word, when we listen too much to the media for our points of truth. For example, I have watched things being prophesied that were not from Heaven's perspective because they spent too much time forming their opinions and political viewpoints based on what they heard on the news or what other people are saying.

As we mentioned concerning Y2K at the beginning of this chapter, fear gripped the hearts of people who believed the world was supposed to come to a crashing halt. The prognostications and prophecies from the second heaven and the earth produced this fear and caused wrong and false prophecies. This was due to where the information was coming from and the spirit that was behind it. This caused some prophecies to be spoken based on fear, anxiety, and panic, taking many in the direction of those words.

Now, that doesn't mean that God won't or doesn't warn us, but it is never driven by a contrary spirit or source. God is not a spirit of fear or panic. He is the Spirit of power, love, and soundness of mind (see 2 Tim. 1:7). Sure, words of warning or judgments may cause one to feel fearful, but it is a healthy fear that causes us to turn to God. It is not a spirit of fear that binds us, consumes us, and causes us to take our eyes off of Him and place them on the thing we are fearing.

We can see from Scripture that the Throne Room prophets were often speaking contrary to what was happening in the earth or culture. One such example is found with Micaiah in the book of First Kings. He's often referred to as the 401st prophet, because after the 400 prophets of Ahab had spoken he was the only prophet who had the true word of the Lord from the Throne Room. He wasn't concerned with being popular, promoted, or appearing powerful in order to be accepted by the king. In fact, King Ahab didn't like him because he never prophesied the things the king wanted to hear. This is what marked him as a Throne Room prophet and not a prophet of the land. He spoke for the one true King of Kings and Lord of Lords from the Throne Room, the third heaven. He didn't speak what was popular in the culture of the earth or pull hell's agenda into existence from the second heaven. Again, this is a reminder of how we discern true from wrong or false. If we take time to observe what the culture is bending toward and the spirit behind that bending, we will see the realm that is influencing the culture trend the most.

We often see in the Bible where genuine prophets were not influenced by the first and second heaven and didn't go along with public opinion, what was popular, or the cultural trends of the day. If the people were partying, sinning, and living wrong, the prophets were weeping and bringing words of repentance and change. If the people were weeping and turning to the Lord, the prophet would bring words of hope and restoration. In the same way, when the world goes the direction of evil or its perspective is contrary to the Lord, we can accurately discern what is the voice of the Lord and what is not.

Another thing we must be aware of when discerning prophecy or prophets is the negative demonic influence of the second heaven, where the occult and warfare realm exists. We must not pull those words or demonic agendas from the second heaven and call it God's voice or will. This is the danger of prophets and prophecy getting caught up in different forms of predicting rather than forthtelling, as a prophet will do. Prediction is based on chance, while forthtelling is based upon revelation, unction, insight, and anointing by the Spirit of God. Psychics operate in this realm of the second heaven and use it to affect those in the earth realm. They are given to prediction. We as prophets are not called to the office of prediction, but rather as those who forthtell by what Heaven reveals, not because man wants the latest bullet points on future events.

Where this has become a real danger is with regard to political elections. Many prophetic vessels spend time predicting who will win an election, rather than forthtelling what God's agenda is. When we first focus on God's agenda, then we can discern who fits the description and purpose of the Lord. Too many things are being prophesied and believed from the second heaven influence. How do we know? This influence is usually found in what become hot button issues that divide, foster hate, and oppose God's agenda, sadly without many even knowing it because they are deceived and blinded by the effects of this second realm. The god of this world, the prince of the power of the air, has blinded their minds from seeing God's perspective and agenda.

The reason fear is so dangerous is because it comes from a spirit contrary to the Lord. Think about how many things are predicted to happen that never do, which cause fear and panic in the earth. Sure, it might have been stopped by prayer, and when we hear such words we should always pray. But how much material has been produced about fearful events that have never taken place? We first have to acknowledge that fear sells. What I mean is that people are geared to tune into predictions about some impending doom or another. We must consider, however, if such material really benefits the listener if it is lacking God's prophetic agenda and plan to help people in the midst of such events. Other than respond in fear, what are hearers supposed to do with information about some apocalyptic event? Just because someone teaches Bible prophecy doesn't mean they stand in the office of a prophet. Just because a person can discern the times, predict certain things, or turn news headlines into prophecies doesn't mean they are receiving and speaking from the Throne Room or have been given that office to forthtell. This doesn't mean prophecy teachers don't have their place, and many of them do tap into prophetic revelation. However, we also need prophets who can reveal the redemptive purposes of God and not just detail and predict fearful end-time events.

Fear creates a lot of confusion because it is part of the demonic agenda of the second realm (see 1 Cor. 14:33). The enemy is always looking for ways to devour those in the earth through doing and saying things contrary to what the Lord is doing or saying. He creates confusion, fear, and entices people to go along with what the majority says and believes, especially through the media. Sadly, the media plays a major role in formulating in people's minds what is acceptable and what is not, what is of God and what is not. The problem is that so often what the world accepts is very contrary to what the Lord does. This results in some people becoming convinced something is being endorsed by the Lord simply because everyone is doing it or saying it.

The prophet Elijah boldly confronted the popular opinion of culture by asking, "Why are you caught between two opinions?"

> *And Elijah came unto all the people, and said, How long halt ye between two opinions? if the Lord be God, follow him: but if Baal, then follow him. And the people answered him not a word* (1 Kings 18:21).

He addressed them this way because prophets of Baal were false prophets of the land. They were trying to mix the worship of Jehovah God with other false gods, thus creating confusion. It took a Throne Room prophet to come and show the people the source and the difference between the words being spoken and what was truly coming from the Throne Room.

False mixtures like with the false prophets of Baal are at work in our day. There have been far too many false mixtures of words being formulated from the earth realm or the second heaven that are supposed to be from God. This mixture brings confusion and division because these prophecies are combined with information and revelation from the first and second realms and then attributed to the Lord. It is those like Elijah who represent the Throne Room who will bring authority, words, and actions that are backed up by Heaven's witness. This is what happened when Elijah prophesied, and he said "at my word it shall not rain."

> *And Elijah the Tishbite, who was of the inhabit-*
> *ants of Gilead, said unto Ahab, As the Lord God of*
> *Israel liveth, before whom I stand, there shall not be*
> *dew nor rain these years, but according to my word*
> (1 Kings 17:1).

Again, when he said, *"the God that answereth by fire, let him be God,"* the Lord backed it up (1 Kings 18:24).

How does this apply to us today? We, too, will be able to accurately discern words or things by whether they have the Lord's backing, witness, and manifestation. In other words, what the genuine prophets say will happen, and you won't be able to deny its source or the realm from which it came. We will clearly know whether it is of the Lord or not. This is why wanting true Throne Room prophets to just spend their time predicting events is wrong and unbiblical. It doesn't mean they won't reveal things to come, but it is through forthtelling, not prediction. Prophets who get into the prediction game fall into the race of who can prophesy the most accurate, specific, and earth-shaking words first and draw the greatest public "wow" factor. What is the danger of prediction-based prophetic? The answer is, it can tap wrongfully and falsely into the second realm of the occult where psychic prediction resides.

Another danger is a true prophet will fall into the need to perform rather than waiting on the Lord to know whether he is to release the prophetic word or not. The longer we walk with the Lord and the more He reveals to us, the less we are allowed to tell and the more carefully we must steward what we receive. When we are secure in our relationship with the Lord, we need not fall into the trap of prediction and feeling like we always have to have a word.

Make it a practice to really pay attention to what you feel and sense when you hear "prophetic" words. When the third heaven is speaking, your spirit will know and your soul will be refreshed! However, when it comes from the second heaven it will feel off and even evil, making you uncomfortable. Now, when words are coming from a person's own soul or flesh, it will come off odd, strange, and will affect you in a negative way. It will give you an uneasy feeling. When words from the second heaven and the earth realm are taken as true words from Heaven, it will bring a sense a fear, panic, evil, and anxiety. Yet words from the Throne Room are filled with authority, power, peace, and will always carry God's redemptive plan of help and hope for mankind and this planet!

Remember, prophets today will minister hope with their warnings if the Lord is truly speaking to and through them. They will offer solutions in the midst of confusion and their prophecies will bring edification, comfort, and exhortation. They will get their information from the third heaven and forthtell Heaven's plans through a healthy filtering of their soul, prophesying words that restore hope, a future, and an expectant end (see Jer. 29:11)!

Chapter Five

THRONE ROOM CLARITY AND PROPHETIC ACCURACY

> *"And he that sat was to look upon like a jasper and a
> sardine [sardis] stone: and there was a rainbow round
> about the throne, in sight like unto an emerald."*
> —Revelation 4:3

In this chapter we will delve further into the question of whether or not genuine prophets can ever miss it, or must they always be 100 percent accurate? This is one of the largest misconceptions surrounding the prophetic. As we mentioned, people commonly believe that a prophet or anyone who prophesies can never make a mistake. Many also believe that

if anyone *does* miss it or prophesies something that doesn't come to pass, they are automatically a false prophet. This is commonly seen across social media platforms where people comment and label various prophetic vessels as false prophets. They do this either because a prophetic word didn't come to pass, or perhaps they wrongly assumed it didn't come to pass and they conclude that the one who spoke is false.

I will begin by saying that the term *false*, when it comes to the prophetic, is tossed around far too loosely. How do we know? Because this term isn't used so quickly when it comes to pastors or teachers who also make honest mistakes in what they communicate. But when it comes to prophets, the term "false" is often used with ease. The truth is, no honest person with good intentions wants to hear their name attached to the word *false*! The word carries such a tremendous indictment against one's integrity, and this needs to be addressed if we are going to function properly in prophetic ministry.

In this chapter I want to give plenty of biblical examples for why we should be careful not to label something as false too quickly. Sure, some of the sloppy practices in prophetic circles have not helped. Some individuals want to be recognized so badly in prophetic ministry that they almost say or prophesy just about anything. This becomes very confusing and misleading to listeners as a whole host of contradictory "prophetic" messages get presented. People wonder who and what to believe. Therefore, as we look at biblical examples of prophets who misspoke or whose prophetic words didn't happen exactly as they said, this is not to imply we don't need a very high standard for accuracy. Accuracy should still be paramount, but just because someone misses it does *not* mean they are false. They might be wrong, but not false. We also want to learn how to differentiate between honest and good-hearted prophets, who may be wrong at times, and false prophets, who are intentionally deceptive.

JASPER, SARDIS, AND EMERALD

Before we seek to answer those questions, let's look again at what happened with the apostle John during his heavenly experience. In Revelation 4, he mentions the jasper and sardis stones and the rainbow around the Throne that looked like an emerald. *"A jasper and a sardine stone: and there was a rainbow round about the throne, in sight like unto an emerald"* (Rev. 4:3). When the apostle John was caught up in the Spirit, He was able to see amazing heavenly things and the worship of the heavenly Father on the Throne. It was in that setting that he saw the jasper and sardis stones and the rainbow around the Throne like an emerald.

He also saw a book that was sealed with seven seals and the Lamb, the Lord Jesus Christ, who is worthy to open the book. When you think of such magnificent stones and their brilliance, you quickly picture their reflective nature. From this setting of brilliant stones around the Throne we can glean some key elements that we need when accurately discerning the word of the Lord. It will also help us to discern genuine prophets and prophecy from the false.

First, these stones and emerald color of the rainbow have a unique prophetic meaning and purpose that point to what must mark every Throne Room prophet and believer. You see, these stones and emerald color not only reflect the Lord's countenance and image but also represent His message. Their reflective, brilliant nature communicates His entire being! These reflections must become ours as well as we reflect Him.

> *But we all, with open face beholding as in a glass the glory of the Lord, are changed into the same image from glory to glory, even as by the Spirit of the Lord* (2 Corinthians 3:18).

It is interesting to note that when Jesus revealed Himself to John, John did not describe His human or natural characteristics, but rather His spiritual characteristics that were full of brilliant light reflected in His countenance. When we read Revelation 4, it is obvious that John was deeply impacted by the brilliance of light and color that radiates from the Lord's appearance.

All three of these things that John saw are heavenly Throne Room characteristics that all Throne Room prophets must have and emulate, both in their messages and their character. It was as though John was recording what God looks like based on His brilliance and countenance, comparing His countenance to the jasper stone and His character, heart, and sacrifice to a sardis stone. He also described the rainbow around the Throne, which was representative of God's nature of love and grace.

These qualities must become our desire and our nature as well and what will mark true prophets. They reveal what is necessary in every prophetic vessel, which false prophets will ignore. What John saw regarding these stones and the emerald color of the rainbow is not just a standard that must be upheld but part of the call to come up higher. Again, these precious stones and color reflect the character, the focus, and even the message of those who minister prophetically and are reminders that will keep us from error. This is where the line separating true from false becomes clearer, because false teachers and prophets were marked by their messages and prophecies as well as their character and behavior.

Let's look more closely at the prophetic meaning of John's description of the Throne Room stones and colors. Scripture says that He who sat on the Throne was like jasper. This color was like a diamond, pure and clear. This is a reference to the Lord and His purity of heart and everything that He is and represents. We find the comparison of the Lord's countenance with the color of jasper recorded in other places as well.

> *Having the glory of God: and her light was like unto a stone most precious, even like a jasper stone, clear as crystal* (Revelation 21:11).

Jasper is like a diamond, which represents the purity of our lives, character, motives, and heart. For the Throne Room prophet, it speaks of purity of heart, purity of words, purity of life. Our hearts and motives must be pure in everything we do! These are not the characteristics of the false prophet; false prophets aren't focused on emulating Jesus or upholding His standards of purity!

In addition to the jasper stone, John sees the Lord as the color of a sardis stone, which is deep red in appearance. This is a blood-red stone representing the redemptive work of the Cross through Jesus' shed blood. It is because of this precious sacrifice, obedience, and act of love, that we have been redeemed. Our sins are completely forgiven and the plan of redemption was fulfilled in Jesus. This means His redemptive love and His plan of help and hope is being extended to those in the earth today.

Every Throne Room prophet must minister with an understanding that God always has a redemptive plan. What do I mean? God's redemptive plan is a plan of help and a plan of hope in every situation and should be found in every word or revelation given. This is the message, mindset, and prophetic understanding that vessels of the Lord must always carry. When you understand this, it will keep you in the right spirit, temperament, and perspective, and the prophetic words you give will carry that as well. This also includes when the Lord gives a warning, chastening, or judgment. The false prophet is not about offering a message of redemption and hope but rather words that draw you away from the Lord. False prophets tend to draw people to themselves using gimmicks, manipulation, trickeries, flatteries, along with corrupt methods and messages. Immorality is also common to their character. All this is contrary to the message and act of redemption we find in the color of the sardis stone, reflecting the Lord's appearance. Every genuine prophetic minister must also appear as a sardis stone, so to speak, because we are His representation in the earth. We must carry and emulate Jesus' redemptive nature of self-sacrifice that offers hope and help. As long as His Spirit remains on earth, God always has a redemptive plan for mankind and for this planet! This means we don't just prophesy problems mixed with doom and gloom, but we prophesy solutions filled with His hope and His help in the midst of the trials, problems, and chaos in people's lives and in the earth.

John continued by describing an emerald-green rainbow around the Throne. He recorded how the Lord operates in both Heaven and earth by the standard and symbol of the rainbow. Today we understand that the rainbow represents God's goodness displayed upon earth, as we see when He promised to never again flood the entire earth with water (see Gen. 9:15). The rainbow shows us His covenant of grace that is extended to all mankind. Every Throne Room prophet must minister with that grace and that is also how prophetic words must be judged. Whether it's a prophecy we share or one that we hear, it must always be filled with grace.

This is where the functions of the Old and New Testament prophets differ. The function of the New Testament prophet is now under a covenant of grace and we minister according to this grace. The Old Testament prophets, however, did not operate under this grace because Jesus had not yet come to establish this covenant of grace by His shed blood. This is why the false prophets and sinful people were stoned in the Old Testament but not in the New Testament. We must be continually reminded of the emerald green color of the rainbow. It is not just a symbol but a reminder that we are to test or judge the prophets according to this covenant of grace, not with harsh judgment. This is the New Testament standard— not the Old Testament standard of the law, which was stoning.

Again, God doesn't deal with His prophets or His people according to the Old Testament law, but by His grace. Today individuals obviously aren't physically stoned, but unfortunately people still hurl verbal stones through harsh, mean-spirited, critical, and judgmental words. Just as we wouldn't throw a physical stone today, we also shouldn't throw stones with our words against others or against God's prophets, regardless of whether we agree with them or not.

The Scripture reminds us that we know in part and we all prophesy in part, meaning we don't know everything. It shows that as imperfect human vessels, we can miss it or make mistakes in our prophetic utterances. Each of us must carry the humble attitude that we are subject to mistakes even with the best of efforts. It is those who think they know everything and hear everything perfectly who can wind up falling into error and ultimately end up becoming false. It's because they are not self-evaluating, and this leads to pride. Pride is one of the dominant characteristics of a false prophet. A lack of self-evaluation not only opens the door to making ongoing mistakes, but it sets one up to fall into dangerous error. Many who have fallen into this trap are easy to recognize in churches because they will often act as though they know more than the pastor. We all need to keep a humble, teachable spirit—especially those of us who minister in the prophetic.

It also tells us in Scripture that the prophets in the church were to judge the revelations of the prophets. *"Let the prophets speak two or three, and let the other judge"* (1 Cor. 14:29). If it's unacceptable for prophets and prophetic ministers to make the occasional honest mistake, then why would Paul even say that prophecy should be reviewed or judged? Here Paul was making allowance for the human error factor. At the same time, he was also ensuring that a proper safeguard was established so God's people would be protected from careless prophetic practices. Also notice that the other person judging or analyzing the prophecy in this verse is referring to another prophet, not any random believer in the church. The prophetic words given in the church setting were evaluated by other seasoned prophets who were recognized by church leadership. They were obviously skilled at evaluating the accuracy and genuineness of the prophetic words being spoken. I believe this is important because if this task was opened to the wider congregation for analysis, it would lead to confusion and likely differing viewpoints and opinions.

The word *judge* in this verse means to weigh, evaluate, and to discern, and this is what other prophets are to do when prophetic words are released, particularly in the church setting where they serve. Now this doesn't mean the average believer cannot test a word or a prophet. We most certainly need to use discernment, especially with the many things that get posted online these days! We should use spiritual discernment and common sense, regardless of whether we are prophets or not. We are all called to exercise our spiritual senses so we can discern between both good and evil (see Heb. 5:14). But this doesn't mean we resort to suspicion and criticism of the prophet because something initially appears as if it didn't come to pass. It may be that the prophetic word spoken needs time to breathe or manifest, and sometimes it can simply be misunderstood by the one hearing or interpreting it.

Of course, vessels or prophets whose inaccurate prophetic words outnumber their accurate ones need to be seen as not speaking for the Lord. Even so, this doesn't automatically make them false. It could be that they need to improve their prophetic practices, and this underscores why we need to know a person's track record and character. However, if all these things do not line up, it shouldn't be hard to make the simple personal decision not to follow them or their words. It's not necessary to get out of the love walk and become unkind in how we respond. We are equally wrong when we point fingers and label someone as false if they aren't false.

We need to reflect and emulate the colors that John saw in the Throne Room. As we do, it will help us in our prophetic ministries and gifting and also in accurately discerning true, wrong, and false prophets and prophecy. Why? Because we will readily recognize the things that do not reflect the Lord's character and truth. When encountering a false prophet, it will be notable because they are tainted by their own pride with themselves as the center focus. Their character isn't one of purity. Even though they may say some accurate things, there will be key elements lacking in their character, revelation, and message. Something about them will lack the reflection of Jesus.

Remember, prophets who do not emulate these three colors that John saw get off track in their character, their message, and the spirit in which they prophesy. They often fall into a situation like Jonah. Jonah was a true prophet of the Lord who prophesied that in forty days Nineveh would be overthrown because of its sinfulness. However, the people repented and God did not overthrow the city. As a result, Jonah's prophetic word didn't come to pass in the way he prophesied it. This made Jonah very angry. Jonah's anger came because God sent him with a prophetic word, but that word never came to pass. Jonah was so upset over it that he wanted to die. Undoubtedly, Jonah wondered what onlookers might have thought and how it may have appeared that he made a mistake. Jonah not only became angry because his word didn't come to pass, he was angry that God extended mercy to Nineveh (see Jonah 4:3). Imagine being angry because God offered someone mercy! Sadly, there are prophetic vessels even today that almost sound as if they want God to judge the world. It often seems this way when they are constantly prophesying God's judgment about almost every situation.

Jonah wasn't a false prophet but a wrong one. He became wrong in his attitude and he focused on himself and his public image. This resulted in him not reflecting the Lord, and he resorted to having a pity party. Jonah could not see the good in the people or rejoice that God had a redemptive plan for the people of Nineveh.

Like Jonah, when our attitude gets off track and we become focused on ourselves, we can fall into the trap of ministering with a wrong spirit. People who do this can only see the bad of a situation, a people, a territory (city or nation) and their bad attitude and words reflect it. Furthermore, they continually prophesy doom and gloom. In effect, they put their hands over their eyes and develop tunnel vision, only seeing *their* burden and the obvious evils of the day. They don't see the bigger, wider perspective or redemptive plan of God like the sardis stone. They forget that God is merciful and is offering hurting humanity His redemptive blood. They also become so focused on their limited perspective that they have forgotten what the rainbow represents, which is God's covenant of grace. This is why every genuine prophetic minister, or believer for that matter, must learn to stay balanced by evaluating themselves honestly and humbly.

Even still, just because a prophet has what I call a "Jonah moment," that doesn't mean they are false. They may just be wrong; but eventually if these wrong attitudes are not dealt with, they can lead to the things that do characterize a false prophet.

This doesn't imply we won't ever receive words from the Throne of coming danger, judgments, or rebukes. It means the scope of what you prophesy and see should not just be always limited to the bad, negative, or evil of the day. On the other hand, the Throne Room prophet must also be willing, like Jonah, to hear and be open to speaking words that will bring the fear of the Lord. They must be willing to speak God's warnings as well and not imply everything will always be a wonderful bed of roses. It is a healthy balance, but the wider view and Spirit that the Lord ministers from is through the lens of His redemptive blood. We must always consider His Spirit of grace and covenant of mercy in every situation when prophesying.

THRONE ROOM CLARITY

We need to give space for the Throne Room prophet to clearly speak and communicate what they are receiving from the Lord under this covenant of grace. What do I mean? Oftentimes the one who is receiving the heart, mind, will, and intent of God will see or hear something but not always understand the whole picture. An example of this was when the apostle John was caught up to the Throne Room and heard, "Behold, the Lion of Judah" but he didn't see a lion. Instead he saw something completely different from what he heard. He saw the Lamb who had been slain.

> *And one of the elders saith unto me, Weep not: behold, the Lion of the tribe of Judah, the Root of David, hath prevailed to open the book, and to loose the seven seals thereof. And I beheld, and, lo, in the midst of the throne and of the four beasts, and in the midst of the elders, stood a Lamb as it had been slain* (Revelation 5:5).

John heard a lion but saw a lamb! This doesn't mean he heard wrong, but this shows us that we can see things and hear things differently and sometimes we need time to get the clarity. It may not be that a prophecy spoken was wrong either. It may just mean there is more to the picture than what we heard or thought the prophetic word was saying. We know that Jesus is *both* the Lion and the Lamb!

This is a good reminder that often what we hear is not always the final picture. This is why it's important to not draw conclusions about a prophecy or prophet too quickly. There may be other pieces to what you heard and it may be different from what you initially perceived. It also means that what we hear takes longer to perceive than what we see, because it takes us longer to identify an object by our hearing or sensing, whereas it takes only a few seconds to identify an object by sight.

When a Throne Room prophet says things like "I perceive" or "I feel," it may be because they sense what the Lord is trying to show or tell them, but they may need more clarity or understanding. We should not be too quick to deem them or their words erroneous. Not only does the prophetic vessel need clarity to what they are hearing, but so does the person receiving the prophecy. A genuine prophetic vessel will always desire Throne Room clarity when prophesying. Their desire is not to miss it or be falsely accused, knowing there are those who are too quick to judge something as being inaccurate.

Remember, the one who prophesies does so according to the measure of their faith. If they or their prophetic words are being judged too quickly as false, this could affect how and what they prophesy going forward. In other words, it may affect them in a negative way by bringing insecurities and reluctance. True Throne Room prophets want to represent the Lord correctly. Due to excessive criticism by those who do not have Throne Room clarity, prophets can be pressured not to step out and give prophetic words from the Lord. It can affect their faith level regarding what they hear, see, or perceive, and even affect their accuracy. They may receive something from the Lord but will hold back for fear of being wrongly accused of speaking an inaccurate word.

An example of this is found in the book of Matthew when Jesus said He would have gathered Israel like a mother hen gathers her baby chicks, but couldn't because they stoned the prophets and those sent to them (see Matt. 23:37). The prophets' words were not received because those who heard their words lacked Throne Room clarity in understanding what they heard. This ultimately not only affected the prophets but those who rejected them. Because they deemed the prophets' words as false, God's agenda was hindered.

Can you imagine how this must have affected the faith level of the prophets throughout history? They might have looked at how other prophets were treated, and it affected their faith to the point of not stepping out and speaking. They would rather play it safe to not create a mess or be part of one. The Scripture shows us an interesting concept in regard to this, that we can also apply when stepping out to speak the prophetic words we receive. *"Where no oxen are, the crib is clean"* (Prov. 14:4). Notice that things in the stall were clean and safe as long as no oxen were in the stalls. This is what can happen to those who prophesy. There is no mess to clean up when you don't step out or desire to go to another level in prophesying. It's safer not to be misunderstood, persecuted, or accused falsely. Some prophets simply will not want to take a risk because of public opinion or scrutiny. As a result, they play it so safe that they end up with empty words or very little to share. As much as we see a great deal of sloppy prophecy and those who are willing to say almost anything, we are also seeing genuine prophets who are holding back because of the fear of accusation.

It is also why some pastors have gotten into a place of suppressing the prophetic in their churches. Obviously, it's because of the bad behavior of some. However, instead of mentoring, teaching, and activating people under correct authority and leadership, they suppress or won't allow prophecy to flow in their services or among their people. They reason that it is safer that way, with no messes to clean up! Now, this desire, goal, and passion to have clean words, pure words, and not create a mess is the mark of a genuine prophet and believer. It is, however, not the nature of a false prophet, as they create messes and don't care what they mess up or who they hurt in the process. This clearly indicates that the level of the prophetic word has not reached the potential that God wants.

Remember when Jesus turned water into wine and had it submitted to the governor of the feast? As we discussed earlier, this speaks of accountability, as He submitted His first miracle to the one in charge of the wedding feast to do a "taste test," if you will. Today, it is a good pastor or prophetic council or advisors who will "taste test" what we are presenting to be from the Throne Room. They can hold us accountable, encourage us, or protect us by giving wisdom and caution to the things we receive from the Lord. This will cause the faith level and measure to arise in the prophetic vessel. When this happens, it will take them to a higher level in what they are receiving from the Lord because they are welcoming accountability and a support system that is not afraid to say, "hey, wait on that," "that is good," or "that tastes awful!"

TESTING PROPHETIC WORDS

In understanding prophetic clarity, we need to briefly discuss how to test prophetic words. Before we deem a prophecy or a prophet as being false, we need to do what the Scripture says—to try or test the spirit of the prophetic word.

> *Beloved, believe not every spirit, but try the spirits whether they are of God: because many false prophets are gone out into the world. Hereby know ye the Spirit of God: Every spirit that confesseth that Jesus Christ is come in the flesh is of God: and every spirit that confesseth not that Jesus Christ is come in the flesh is not of God: and this is that spirit of antichrist, whereof ye have heard that it should come; and even now already is it in the world* (1 John 4:1-3).

First, every prophetic word needs to be tested by the word of God, the final authority for testing all prophecy. Prophetic words don't add or take away from the Bible; rather, they are backed up by the Scriptures and right doctrine.

Second, a word from God will carry the Spirit's witness with our spirit because the word is coming from the Lord. If being spoken through a true prophet, and if it's from the Lord, it should carry weight, authority, and anointing. If the prophecy is being spoken through a believer who is not a prophet, your spirit should still bear witness with a peace or a sense of spiritual confirmation that it's coming from the Lord. I am not saying the word has to always confirm something you already know; rather, there is confirmation by a sense of agreement that we feel in our spirit. It should bring an uplifting witness in our spirit that edifies, exhorts, and comforts us.

When accurately discerning a prophecy, it is important to not just discern the words that were spoken but also the source or spirit behind the one speaking. This will help to better determine if the word is coming from the Lord, the person delivering the word, or an evil spirit. Always remember just because a word may be accurate doesn't mean it is coming from the Lord. As we will consider further in this chapter, false prophets were known for some of their prophecies being accurate, or they wouldn't have misled the people. In addition, the enemy *does* and *can* appear as an angel of light, deceiving many with accurate words, revelations, and experiences. This is why we need to discern both the vessel and source speaking through them as well as the word prophesied.

The apostle Paul is a good New Testament example of discerning prophecy and the ones delivering the prophetic words. He had a young girl following him with a spirit of divination or witchcraft who was speaking accurate things. Yet after a while of hearing these sayings, Paul discerned or felt in his own heart that even though the words were true, the source or spirit behind them wasn't! The source of the words this young girl was speaking was an evil spirit.

> *And it came to pass, as we went to prayer, a certain damsel possessed with a spirit of divination met us, which brought her masters much gain by soothsaying: the same followed Paul and us, and cried, saying, These men are the servants of the most high God, which shew unto us the way of salvation. And this did she many days. But Paul, being grieved,*

> *turned and said to the spirit, I command thee in*
> *the name of Jesus Christ to come out of her. And he*
> *came out the same hour* (Acts 16:16-18).

Third, before deeming a prophecy as false or wrong, we should always remember the importance of timing when a word is spoken and the importance of having correct interpretation of it. Throne Room clarity keeps us from putting our own interpretation on the prophetic word. This is especially true with prophetic words that have to do with timing, as we mentioned. Many prophets of old and even today are mistakenly labeled as false because of a wrong interpretation of their prophecy or because the timing didn't seem to play out as spoken. An example of this would be all the prophets of the Bible who spoke words that they thought would happen in their lifetime but didn't.

A true prophet will anguish over the words given them. In other words, they deeply care about how hearers are affected by the words they speak. However, an immature, undisciplined, and even false prophet will not do so. True prophets and believers who desire to prophesy genuinely are more concerned about the Lord's heart being correctly represented and communicated. How does this affect the people whom we are delivering the word to? We want to make sure it is in the right spirit and delivered correctly so it doesn't bring dishonor to the Lord, the word, or the vessel giving it. This is why a genuine prophet will be slower to deliver a word and have a certain caution. He or she will have a holy respect and fear before delivering the words of the Lord. This is all part of the anguish of the prophet and will include possible misunderstanding, mis-treatment, and even spiritual opposition that comes with the prophetic word. A false prophet is unlikely to anguish over these things as they are not connected to the heart of God or His truth. Understanding this will help us to receive greater Throne Room clarity when discerning a prophetic word, and it will correctly mark a true prophet who *will* anguish over the word of the Lord that they give.

The Anguish of a True Prophet

Let's look further into the subject of the anguish of a true prophet. When a prophet truly fears the Lord, they can experience a sense of anguish in processing the words they receive from Him. This anguish comes out of a deep sense of always wanting to correctly represent the Lord and the words He gives. A prophet can experience a sense of anguish as they process the words given due to fearing the Lord because they are careful to represent Him and the word correctly. They can sometimes feel the opposition, responsibility, backlash, and misunder-standing of them and the word they carry. This is especially true when the word the Lord has spoken to them goes against what they reasoned or is completely opposite of what people believe or want to hear. The anguish becomes an inner tug-of-war or even wrestling as to whether the word is correct. Did they receive it correctly and is it supported by Scripture? How is it going to be received? Is it going to be understood, misinterpreted, or judged incorrectly? Will it stir up natural and spiritual opposition that no one knows or understands but the prophet who spoke it? Will this word prophesied cause the prophet to be mislabeled and judged harshly? In the end, will the prophet be vindicated by the word given?

Jeremiah was one such prophet who anguished over the words that the Lord gave him. His anguish clearly shows what a genuine prophet will oftentimes go through when the Lord gives them a word.

> *Oh, my anguish, my anguish! I writhe in pain. Oh, the agony of my heart! My heart pounds within me, I cannot keep silent. For I have heard the sound of the trumpet; I have heard the battle cry* (Jeremiah 4:19 NIV).

This is just a small glimpse of the anguish that comes from the prophet's inner dealings with the Lord and the rehearsing of the words prophesied, especially when they are not popular in public opinion. Yet this is the price of the prophetic anointing and office given by Jesus.

This anguish is what marks a true prophet from those who are not. The mere fact that they are even anguishing at all over the word of the Lord is a proving sign. This is a great safety check and reminder of the One we represent and how important His words are. A true prophet never wants to misrepresent the Lord or His anointing and giftings and never desires to hurt the people to whom they minister the word of the Lord. A false prophet never anguishes but often brags, gloats, and refuses to humble themselves concerning the prophecies they speak. False prophets don't anguish over the words they share because they don't hold the Lord and His heart with honor or respect.

Remember, prophesying accurate words that come to pass is vital, but it is not necessarily what fully identifies a true prophet from a false prophet. Definitions are often formulated by the ideals and expectations. Many define either a true or false prophet based on whether they prophesy things that come to pass or not. They are labeled as true prophets if they had an accurate word and never miss it. People commonly differentiate true from false based on accuracy, and if someone is 100 percent accurate then they must be a true prophet. This ideology simply isn't reliable. One failed prophecy does not mean a prophet is false any more than perfect accuracy makes one genuine. Again, as we have been discussing, their character is the first factor on whether they are true or false.

On the matter of accurate versus inaccurate prophecy, I do want to go back for further review of the story of Samuel. As I mentioned, this is probably the most common example people use to support the belief that prophets cannot ever make a mistake. Let's look at this example from Scripture more closely.

SAMUEL'S WORDS

I regularly hear people say, "We want accurate prophets today who are like Samuel, whose words never fell to the ground!" While having prophetic accuracy is important, we also must not imply that somehow the Old Testament prophets were more anointed, better, or more accurate than those in the New Testament. We also shouldn't think that even the genuine prophets of the Bible were faultless or without error.

Now, let's consider why the Bible says that Samuel's words never fell to the ground. Does it mean he never missed it and was 100 percent accurate in every prophetic utterance given? Should this be the rule for all who prophesy?

As we touched on in the previous chapter, it seems that Samuel went to the house of Jesse with some of his own preconceived ideas or biases. Remember, the prophetic word he was carrying was to go to the house of Jesse and anoint one of his sons to be the next king of Israel.

> *Now the Lord said to Samuel, "How long will you mourn for Saul, seeing I have rejected him from reigning over Israel? Fill your horn with oil, and go; I am sending you to Jesse the Bethlehemite. For I have provided Myself a king among his sons"* (1 Samuel 16:1 NKJV).

Like every person who prophesies, this prophetic word still had to be filtered through Samuel's own mind, will, and emotions. We can see how this could have been true when he thought the oldest son, Eliab, would be the most likely candidate for king, based on the fact that the firstborn son carried the right of inheritance. He certainly looked the part. Samuel began to speak that Eliab was the Lord's anointed whom he would anoint as king.

> *And it came to pass, when they had come, that he looked on Eliab and said, "Surely the Lord's anointed is before Him"* (1 Samuel 16:6 KJ21).

These words Samuel spoke were not the Lord's but his own. These words didn't mean Samuel was false or even knew everything; he had to process the prophetic word the Lord had spoken so he could minister the prophecy accurately.

It took several times of Jesse's sons passing before him to process the word of the Lord regarding the one the Lord had chosen.

> *So Jesse called Abinadab, and made him pass before Samuel. And he said, "Neither has the Lord chosen this one." Then Jesse made Shammah pass by. And he said, "Neither has the Lord chosen this one." Thus Jesse made seven of his sons pass before Samuel. And Samuel said to Jesse, "The Lord has not chosen these"* (1 Samuel 16:8-10 NKJV).

In each case, until it was revealed that David was the Lord's anointed, he still had to process the prophetic word though his own human soul.

However, as Samuel looked upon the firstborn son, Eliab, the Lord told him this was not His anointed and instructed him to not judge by outward appearance.

> *But the Lord said unto Samuel, Look not on his countenance, or on the height of his stature; because I have refused him: for the Lord seeth not as man seeth; for man looketh on the outward appearance, but the Lord looketh on the heart* (1 Samuel 16:7).

This is where genuine prophets and those who prophesy can make mistakes. It is important to avoid allowing our minds or preconceived ideas about something or someone to cause us to miss it. Samuel started to anoint Eliab until the Lord stopped him. Although he eventually heard which son was to be anointed, he was initially on the wrong path and it took a divine interruption to redirect him.

I remember once hearing a prophetic word in my heart concerning a specific woman the Lord was showing me in the audience. The prophetic word I heard was she had just recently lost her husband and was now a widow, and she was really grieving his departure. Yet when I looked at her my mind didn't line up with the word I heard. She looked happy, had a huge diamond on the ring finger of her left hand, and to make it more challenging she was sitting next to a man who looked like he was her husband. Nevertheless, I tread on what I thought was risky ground. I decided to step out and deliver the word in the form of a question. I asked, "Have you recently become a widow?" She immediately burst into tears and began sobbing. I ministered the word to her and later was briefed by the pastor that the man sitting next to her was a relative who brought her to the meeting because her husband had just died, and she was grieving terribly.

The same was true for Samuel at the house of Jesse—his mind was telling him one thing as the prophetic word came to him. As a result, he spoke out thinking Eliab, the firstborn, was the one God was choosing. Samuel was not being a false prophet. He was simply processing the prophetic word through his mind, as all prophets and prophetic people have to do. He wasn't 100 percent right, nor did he know everything. Yet his spirit, his character, and his words could be trusted by those who heard them—even to the point that they feared his name and his coming into a city.

> *So Samuel did what the Lord said, and went to Bethlehem. And the elders of the town trembled at his coming, and said, "Do you come peaceably?"* (1 Samuel 16:4 NKJV)

This same trustworthiness and reliability should be true of us. We may have human error from time to time in our prophetic gifting or prophecies. The difference between what makes it false, wrong, or true is our intention. The intention of our hearts will clearly differentiate what is false from an honest mistake. However, just like with Samuel, our track record needs to be more dependable and accurate than not. The majority of our prophetic words should line up and reveal a genuine prophet or prophecy more than the minority of words that show otherwise.

If Samuel had to process the prophetic words he received just like we all do, what does it mean when the Bible says his words never fell to the ground? I believe upon further consideration and looking at this phrase within its context we will see that his words not falling to the ground carried a much larger purpose. It was not so much about Samuel being a prophet without human imperfections, but rather about the era and time of history in which he was called to prophesy.

If having perfect accuracy, or one's "words never falling to the ground," is the requirement or measuring stick for all true prophets and prophecy, then we just indicated that every other prophet in Scripture was a false prophet. Think about it.

The Bible never says their words didn't fall to the ground. It only says this of Samuel. However, the other prophets of the Bible were also true prophets. To use what the Scripture says of Samuel's words as a prophetic measuring stick for discerning between true and false prophets would discount or even falsify prophets such as Jonah, Micah, Nahum, Elijah and Elisha, Jeremiah, Isaiah, and many others.

When Scripture says Samuel's words didn't fall to the ground, it points to several things that were happening and needed at the time of his prophetic calling and assignment.

First, Eli the priest was allowing corruption in the priesthood on the front steps of the temple by his sons, who committed sexual immorality with women. This defiled the priesthood and the temple because Eli did not do anything is stop it. This required a prophet and prophetic words that would not only confront the issue but bring things into divine order. Samuel would be used as a prophet who heard from the Lord and would reestablish divine order in the house of the Lord.

Second, we must consider that the Lord's word to Samuel had to be upheld because of who Samuel was and what he was called to prophesy. He was called to declare that the Messiah would come and be seated upon the Throne of David. David would have to be appointed and chosen correctly, because he was instrumental in bringing forth the lineage of the Messiah. Samuel's words had to be carefully watched over by the Lord. The very lineage of the Messiah was at stake and how He would come forth could not fall to the ground! This historic prophetic assignment was given to Samuel because of his precise track record in hearing the voice of the Lord. It didn't mean Samuel never had to filter the words through his own emotions before he delivered them. The Lord saw to it that Samuel's words and conduct would be trustworthy. Not only that, but the Lord also ensured Samuel was raised up as a respectable and honorable man, since he'd been trained as a young boy under Eli, a corrupt priest and mentor.

Third, we must consider the whole verse and not just the latter part. *"And Samuel grew, and the Lord was with him, and did let none of his words fall to the ground"* (1 Sam. 3:19). As we can see from this verse, Samuel *grew up*—meaning, from the time his parents entrusted him to Eli the priest, the Lord was watching over his prophetic process, maturity, and prophetic words. It was not just his words that would have to be upheld, but a combination of his character, integrity, morals, and maturity as he was growing in the midst of a corrupt environment. If you recall, at that time people were being taken advantage of under the priesthood of Eli and his sons, and the Lord had to exonerate Samuel in a special way. God ensured Samuel's words would never be discarded and discounted by those who would witness them. It was important for people to see that Samuel was unique and not like the corruption under which he served. God upheld Samuel's words carefully so the lineage of the Messiah could be established in the midst of this immoral environment. God carefully saw to it that Samuel would be known as a trustworthy and pure prophet who did not partake in the sinful practices of those around him. It is all very similar to the way the Lord watched over the prophetic destinies of Moses and Jesus when they were born, protecting them from Pharaoh and Herod so the purposes of God would not be aborted.

Samuel's words would not be hindered, compromised, or aborted because of what was at stake. Again, this is not saying he could never miss it, nor is it saying that no prophet could ever make a mistake. This further underscores why, when discerning a prophetic word, we have to be careful not to be too quick to label a prophetic minister or prophecy false or wrong. We live in a microwave society that wants everything now, including prophecies. Yet there are many prophetic words from the prophets of old that are still coming to pass even now, centuries later. Some were accused falsely in their day because people misinterpreted the timing of their words. As a result of misinterpretation, they were often deemed false and even stoned. In the same way, we do a disservice to prophetic ministers when we jump on the bandwagon of accusation. We must be intentional about seeking the Lord anytime we hear prophecies and prophetic words, knowing that if a word has truly come from the Lord, He will be faithful to bring it to pass.

TESTING PROPHETS AND PROPHECY

So, if it's possible that prophets and those who prophesy *can* make the occasional honest mistake, then how are we to handle such situations? Matthew 7 tells us that we will recognize false prophets by their fruit. If we can recognize a false prophet by their fruit, then we can recognize those who are *not* false prophets by their fruit as well.

> *Beware of false prophets, which come to you in sheep's clothing, but inwardly they are ravening wolves. Ye shall know them by their fruits. Do men gather grapes of thorns, or figs of thistles? Even so every good tree bringeth forth good fruit; but a corrupt tree bringeth forth evil fruit. A good tree cannot bring forth evil fruit, neither can a corrupt tree bring forth good fruit. Every tree that bringeth not forth good fruit is hewn down, and cast into the fire. Wherefore by their fruits ye shall know them* (Matthew 7:15-20).

Here are a few things to consider when you hear a prophetic word that you're not sure about. Consider the person giving the word, and ask yourself these questions:

- Do they reflect the character and integrity of God in other areas of their life?
- What is their track record (have they given accurate words in the past)?
- How do you know the prophecy is wrong?

If you see the nature of God in them and they have a solid history of accurate words, consider that they may have made a mistake or possibly that the word itself may take time to come to pass. This person is not a false prophet, but simply a person who's perhaps made an honest mistake.

Also, be careful *how* you hear. As we've discussed throughout this book, human error is involved in both the one who gives the word *and* the one who hears the word. It is always wise to lay prophetic words before the Lord, asking Him for interpretation and understanding. Consult the Scripture to make sure what was spoken aligns with God's Word. In our "microwave" world, we want all the answers now, but it often takes time for words to unfold and come to pass. It is always worth taking the time to search the Scripture and seek the heart of the Lord!

> *It is the glory of God to conceal a thing: but the honour of kings is to search out a matter* (Proverbs 25:2).

Most importantly, it is critical that we stay in the Spirit and not become carnal in our reactions to the words we hear. When we are quick to react in our flesh, we actually side with the enemy in bringing division and discord. This does much more damage to the Body of Christ than we often realize. It is never appropriate to assassinate someone's character because we don't agree with the words they speak. If, and when, prophets (and those who minister prophetically) make honest mistakes and we harshly judge and criticize them, we can shut ourselves off from the voice of God. Although this may not be our intention, this attitude of our heart rejects not only the person speaking but the Lord, who has entrusted them to speak His words.

Again, we need to remember that the primary characteristic of a false prophet is found in their intention and character.

Having this clear understanding will help us better recognize and handle those who have perhaps made an honest mistake. If someone is a false prophet, we will likely see evidence that their primary activity is leading people astray, whether doctrinally, financially, or for some other purpose. This is how the Bible describes the false prophet.

> *If there arise among you a prophet, or a dreamer of dreams, and giveth thee a sign or a wonder, and the sign or the wonder come to pass, whereof he spake unto thee, saying, Let us go after other gods, which thou hast not known, and let us serve them; thou shalt not hearken unto the words of that prophet, or that dreamer of dreams: for the Lord your God proveth you, to know whether ye love the Lord your God with all your heart and with all your soul. Ye shall walk after the Lord your God, and fear him, and keep his commandments, and obey his voice, and ye shall serve him, and cleave unto him. And that prophet, or that dreamer of dreams, shall be put to death; because he hath spoken to turn you away from the Lord your God, which brought you out of the land of Egypt, and redeemed you out of the house of bondage, to thrust thee out of the way which the Lord thy God commanded thee to walk in. So shalt thou put the evil away from the midst of thee* (Deuteronomy 13:1-5).

Notice in verses 1 and 2 that the prophet had dreams and miracles that actually *did* come to pass. In other words, they gave accurate prophetic revelations, but they were still a false prophet. It wasn't about their accuracy; it was about their intent to deceive.

Think for a moment why there would have to be certain elements or segments of a false prophet's words and prophetic revelations that would have accuracy to them. If it was obvious that everything they were saying *wasn't* true, people wouldn't be deceived. So, there is more than accuracy that we need to consider.

First, can you discern the source behind their prophesying? If you don't know the person, again, pay attention to how their words make you feel. Do you have an uneasiness in your spirit? If it is a genuine word from the Lord, even though the delivery or their appearance may feel uncomfortable, you will have a witness or an "agreement" in your spirit. Also, does what they are saying line up with the Word of God?

If they aren't a legitimate prophet, then obviously it wasn't the Lord who was speaking but rather it was their own spirit or perception that was involved. In some cases, it was an evil spirit giving them insights. The Bible calls these spirits familiar spirits. Familiar spirits take on something familiar, or something that you would recognize. A familiar spirit is a demon that is summoned by a medium with the intent that the spirit summoned will obey his or her commands. Often, familiar spirits are believed to be the spirits of people who have died (see Deut. 18:11). However, biblically this is not the case. Such appearances are actually demonic forces imitating people in order to deceive.

Another way familiar spirits operate is by watching and becoming familiar with information that is revealed in the natural realm, not by supernatural revelation from God. Now, this is not to say that our human ability to perceive things means that we are tapping into the demonic realm. We can often perceive things naturally, but it's important to let others know what we've observed on our own and what we've heard from the Lord. This will eliminate confusion regarding the source of revelation.

People operating in the realm of familiar spirits usually know they're doing it and are manufacturing "revelation." These evil spirits are revealing something from what they have observed about another person or situation. It's important to mention that when people don't rely on the Holy Spirit and operate in this kind of manufactured knowledge, they are opening a door into the demonic realm. They are receiving accurate information, but it is coming from a demonic source, not from the Lord. Though operating this way may seem harmless at first, once this door has been opened, the enemy will not hesitate to rush in and overtake the person if they choose to continue their practices. When this happens, the person is on their way to becoming a false prophet, as their motives are becoming manipulative and self-seeking rather than pure and God-seeking.

Second, what separated a false prophet from a wrong prophet in the Bible was the fruit of his life and message that drew the people away from the Lord and into serving other gods. He drew their love and attention away from God. It was this type of false prophet who was to be put to death. Continue to note that it was not so much based on the accuracy of their prophetic words, as we saw in Deuteronomy 13:1-2. Notice the reason why this false prophet who had accurate words was stoned.

> *And that prophet, or that dreamer of dreams, shall be put to death; because he hath spoken to turn you away from the Lord your God* (Deuteronomy 13:5).

The false prophet was stoned because they were intentionally deceiving the people through their accurate prophetic words and revelations, which drew people away from God.

This is why stoning wasn't for the true prophet. Even though they were unfortunately falsely accused, God didn't require the genuine prophet who may have missed it, misspoke, or made an honest mistake to be put to death. Remember how Samuel continued down the line of Jesse's sons after his first mistake. He was not a false prophet because He mistook Eliab as the Lord's anointed—Samuel was simply human! Because Samuel was pure in heart, the Lord stuck close by him and made sure he understood and spoke the word correctly (see 1 Sam. 2:3). God's heart is always toward those whose intentions are good, even when they make mistakes! This is not at all how He deals with false prophets. Though God is a god of mercy, the Bible says His Spirit doesn't always strive with man (see Gen. 6:3). The false prophet intentionally determines to draw others away from the Lord, and the Lord takes this very seriously.

> *Therefore thus says the Lord God: "Because you have spoken nonsense and envisioned lies, therefore*

I am indeed against you," says the Lord God. "My hand will be against the prophets who envision futility and who divine lies; they shall not be in the assembly of My people, nor be written in the record of the house of Israel, nor shall they enter into the land of Israel. Then you shall know that I am the Lord God" (Ezekiel 13:8-9 NKJV).

This is a serious reminder why there must be solid prophetic training. We must help to develop the right character in those who prophesy so they can present pure and accurate prophetic words and stand in the days of testing and persecution. When people are solidly trained, it also gives them credibility with their hearers. Those who hear them prophesy know without question where they've come from and who they are connected with, and this is key to discerning the true from the false. Purposefully deceitful false prophets and, yes, even undisciplined, wrong prophets *do* need to be discerned and discounted, but proper training and development will make the genuine stand out from the false. Jesus said that branches that don't produce good fruit need to be removed, so we must remember that looking at the fruit of a person's life and ministry is essential in drawing the right conclusions.

We should also consider the fact that stoning in the Old Testament was not just limited to false prophets but also included those who committed adultery and other sinful acts under the same law.

The man who commits adultery with another's wife, even his neighbor's wife, the adulterer and the adulteress shall surely be put to death (Leviticus 20:10 AMPC).

In reality, under this same law King David should have been stoned for his adultery with Bathsheba, but he wasn't. We also should have had this same law go into effect concerning Aaron the priest. He actually did what a false prophet does. He drew people away from God to worship a golden calf. The law of God was fresh in Moses' hands as he was coming down the mountain. According to the law Moses had just received, his brother Aaron was now guilty of being a false prophet and punishable by death! The Bible says that Aaron was a prophet.

> *And the Lord said unto Moses, See, I have made thee a god to Pharaoh: and Aaron thy brother shall be thy prophet* (Exodus 7:1).

There was no better time to enforce this law, was there? I find it interesting that Aaron wasn't stoned by Moses or the elders. Why weren't David and Aaron stoned? Perhaps it was because the intentions of their hearts were not to deceive, even though they both did deceive. Remember, man looks at the outward appearance, but God looks on the heart (see 1 Sam. 16:7).

Look further at Deuteronomy 13 about who else was to be stoned as punishment. Notice it was not just the prophet who turned people away from the Lord.

> *If thy brother, the son of thy mother, or thy son, or thy daughter, or the wife of thy bosom, or thy friend, which is as thine own soul, entice thee secretly,*

saying, Let us go and serve other gods, which thou
hast not known, thou, nor thy fathers; namely, of the
gods of the people which are round about you, nigh
unto thee, or far off from thee, from the one end of
the earth even unto the other end of the earth; thou
shalt not consent unto him, nor hearken unto him;
neither shall thine eye pity him, neither shalt thou
spare, neither shalt thou conceal him: but thou shalt
surely kill him; thine hand shall be first upon him
to put him to death, and afterwards the hand of all
the people. And thou shalt stone him with stones,
that he die; because he hath sought to thrust thee
away from the Lord thy God, which brought thee
out of the land of Egypt, from the house of bond-
age. And all Israel shall hear, and fear, and shall do
no more any such wickedness as this is among you
(Deuteronomy 13:6-11).

We can see here that this requirement for stoning or being put to death also applied to *anyone* who simply drew people away from God for any reason! Remember, the false prophets in this chapter of Deuteronomy had accurate words, and the main reason they were stoned was because their character and prophecies purposefully drew people away from the Lord. If they were leading people astray as the prophet did in the previous verses of Deuteronomy 13, the same discipline was to be applied.

It is interesting that when people want to call for a mod-ern-day "stoning" of someone they deem to be a false prophet, they often ignore those in the church who draw people away from the Lord into carnal, sinful living. How about the person who may have tried to draw people away from a good church, a godly pastor, or draw others into things that divide the house of God through gossip, strife, and offense? Typically, we prefer to make church discipline apply to prophets but are less quick to apply our same methods of discipline when things hit closer to home. However, as we saw with Aaron, Moses' brother, he actually did do the things that made him guilty of being a false prophet and he wasn't stoned according to the law. We must be careful not to do the same to genuine prophets and prophetic people today!

As we give and receive prophetic words, let's stay mindful of the fact that we are all human and, therefore, all prone to error. Not every word will be delivered with 100 percent accuracy and clarity. On the other side of the equation, not every word will be *heard* or understood in the way the Lord intends it. We must remember it is not only the one who gives a word who is responsible for it, but the hearer is also responsible to steward their own discernment and understanding of what they've heard.

Remember, whether we are giving or receiving prophecy, we are safe when we stay before the Lord and ask for wisdom and understanding from the Holy Spirit. It is always important to be able to discern true from false and to separate ourselves from that which is not pleasing to the Lord. He has made it very clear that He will deal with those who speak deceitfully and lead people away from Him. The key for us is, no matter what anyone else is doing or saying, we must always remain humble and gentle in how we act toward others, seeking to reflect the heart and nature of the One who sits on the Throne.

Chapter Six

FALSE PROPHETS
AND THRONE ROOM
COUNTERFEITS

> *"And out of the throne proceeded lightnings
> and thunderings and voices: and there were
> seven lamps of fire burning before the throne,
> which are the seven Spirits of God."*
> —REVELATION 4:5

So far, we've looked at several aspects of the apostle John's encounter in Revelation 4, and now I want to focus on what he saw proceeding out of the Throne—lightning, thundering, and voices!

> *And out of the throne proceeded lightnings and
> thunderings and voices: and there were seven lamps*

*of fire burning before the throne, which are the seven
Spirits of God* (Revelation 4:5).

These are three more key prophetic attributes that genuine
prophets and believers must have if they desire to minister in
honor and accuracy before the Lord. It is pure, willing vessels
who allow God to speak words through us like thunder and
display his power like lightning, who preserve His words and
voice in the earth.

The lightning, thundering, and voices from the Throne
caught John's attention. These are the elements found in the
authentic prophetic, but they also represent what false prophets pervert. This is because rather than truly flowing in what
these three attributes prophetically represent, false prophets use them to draw attention to themselves. False prophets
want to steal the thunder from the Lord by sounding and
appearing authoritative and powerful themselves. They desire
to bring attention to themselves and draw others away from
the Lord through lightning-like displays of self, pride, deceit,
and manipulative gimmicks. Rather than seeking to be pure,
anointed vessels from the Throne Room, they want to be the
voice you follow rather than the voice of the Lord.

We are always to honor His thunderous voice and properly
manifest the lightnings of His power! This is not the desire or
an attribute of a false prophet.

This is what separates genuine prophetic ministers from
the false counterfeits. How is that? Again, it goes back to the
intentions of our hearts. A genuine prophet wants to protect
the thunder of God's voice because it is the sound of His heart,

but the false prophet does not hold the heart of God in honor. In addition, the true prophet will handle God's words and power correctly, but the false prophet perverts them through deceit while still acting as though they are greatly anointed. The true prophet wants to manifest the lightnings of God's power humbly and honorably. And just like thunder is the sound that follows the manifestation of lightning, the "thunder" of a genuine prophetic minister is a glorious display of God's voice in honor and power—from a place of humility, not in flashy ways that draw attention to themselves.

The false prophet is all about their own "lightning show" or showboating, constantly letting everyone know how great they are, how powerful they are, and how they can benefit you. This is completely opposite of a genuine prophet who recognizes their power comes from the Lord and they are nothing without Him. Though you are benefited by following the ministry of a genuine prophet, they will ensure that their ministry points you to the Lord. Remember, false prophets want to be the center of attention or on center stage. They desire that their audience be "wowed" and amazed by their gifting and displays of supernatural power, much like lightning, followed by the sounds of thunderous words. This is exactly what false prophets did in the Old Testament—they looked for ways to powerfully draw people to themselves, away from God and into error and counterfeits.

Today's false prophets are identified by what is lacking in their character, morals, methods, message, money handling, and words and behaviors when they minister. They may sound powerful like thunder and even appear genuine and striking like lightning in their voices. Yet over time they are proven to be counterfeits because they deviate from what the Lord intends for them to emulate from the Throne.

When we continue in the revelation given to the apostle John in further chapters, we see something added to what he witnessed in the thunder, lightning, and voices—there was also an earthquake.

> *And the angel took the censer, and filled it with fire of the altar, and cast it into the earth: and there were voices, and thunderings, and lightnings, and an earthquake* (Revelation 8:5).

False prophets will capitalize on methods to get people shaken or moved, to respond to their deceit. They look for creative ways to manipulate and draw people to respond. Now obviously, the genuine prophet wants people to respond and be moved upon, even shaken as well. The difference is the genuine prophet wants this to be a result of the Holy Spirit working through and among them, confirming the word with signs following. But the false prophet's trust is not in the Lord. They don't look to the Lord as their source of inspiration or power to move people. Instead, they resort to falsifying things to make it appear like it is the Lord. We've sometimes seen this happen when those proclaiming to have a prophetic gift research to find information about those they prophesy to. They make it look as if they are getting prophetic words, words of knowledge and wisdom from the Lord, when it's actually prior knowledge that they obtained through their own research. The genuine prophet would rather know nothing from natural observation or research and speak by the Spirit. He or she would rather not prophesy at all if they didn't divinely receive their information from the Lord.

In addition, false prophets will twist the Scriptures to support the acceptance of practices and manifestations that may be unbiblical, false, or in some cases downright immoral. Then they will attempt to call it a "fresh" revelation or move of God. This is often why they will spend most of their time drawing attention to "supernatural" manifestations, but less attention to the importance of Scripture. Also consider that many of their manifestations are much different from those of the early apostles. I believe that is a key sign to look for. They emphasize the "new" and "different" and add emphasis that is beyond the Word of God.

Another way that a false prophet is easily recognized is by how they handle money or how they handle other people's money! Now, we know that Scripture shows us that there is a need for offerings, partnership, and raising of funds to further the Gospel. This should be done, as the Bible says, unto the Lord and not out of compulsion (see 2 Cor. 9:7). However, the false prophet violates these genuine spiritual and financial laws that govern and bring blessings to God's people. Rather than handle God's people with respect and dignity, false prophets, especially in money matters, resort to gimmicks, manipulation, and out-and-out false means to get people to give to them financially.

The thunder, lightning, voices, and earthquakes—the manifestations in ministry—are to cause a human response that results in honor to the Lord and changed lives of those who experience them. They should also cause us to have a greater fear and respect of the Lord. These "lightnings and thunders" are also how the Lord speaks and don't need to be counterfeited, manipulated, or falsified.

This is important because not only does God want to speak, He wants to show His power and cause men to be moved by His Spirit. There are several references in Scripture to the Lord's voice being like thunder and His display of power like lightning, with the result being the shaking of the earth itself.

> *The voice of thy thunder was in the heaven: the lightnings lightened the world: the earth trembled and shook* (Psalm 77:18).

> *Hear attentively the noise of his voice, and the sound that goeth out of his mouth. He directeth it under the whole heaven, and his lightning unto the ends of the earth. After it a voice roareth: he thundereth with the voice of his excellency; and he will not stay them when his voice is heard* (Job 37:2-4).

All of these are to remind us that what proceeds from the Throne is to reveal God's heart that wants to be heard, His love that He desires to demonstrate, and for His people to be drawn closer to Him so they will be blessed abundantly. We find this when God came down upon Mount Sinai to visit the people of Israel under Moses' leadership. It was His voice like thunder and His power displayed like lightning that caused both the earth and the people to tremble.

And it came to pass on the third day in the morning, that there were thunders and lightnings, and a thick cloud upon the mount, and the voice of the trumpet exceeding loud; so that all the people that was in the camp trembled. And Moses brought forth the people out of the camp to meet with God; and they stood at the nether part of the mount. And mount Sinai was altogether on a smoke, because the Lord descended upon it in fire: and the smoke thereof ascended as the smoke of a furnace, and the whole mount quaked greatly (Exodus 19:16-18).

This is exactly what we saw with the apostle John as he witnessed the thunder, the lightning, and earthquakes causing the earth to fear and honor God! This visitation of God upon this mountain is a beautiful picture of what should happen today when true Throne Room prophecy is being uttered. We should be drawn to the Lord because of His words and His beautiful signs and wonders that cause us to desire and honor Him more.

As we see, in this account in the book of Exodus, there is the sound of thunder, which speaks of His voice; lightning, which speaks of His power; and the sound of trumpets, which represents Throne Room prophecy being uttered through our lips. It is interesting to note the shaking that took place when God came down upon Mount Sinai is paralleled in other accounts in the Book of Revelation with the same manifestations.

And the temple of God was opened in heaven, and there was seen in his temple the ark of his testament:

and there were lightnings, and voices, and thunderings, and an earthquake, and great hail (Revelation 11:19).

And there were voices, and thunders, and lightnings; and there was a great earthquake, such as was not since men were upon the earth, so mighty an earthquake, and so great (Revelation 16:18).

These examples not only remind us of God visiting Moses and the people upon the mountain but reveal to us exactly what happens when God's voice thunders through true prophecy and His genuine prophetic vessels. The result should be a moving of the Lord upon the people that brings them to a proper response so that they will know that the Lord, who sits on the Throne, is the source of the words you speak! They will sense it, feel it, and know it, just like with the three elements of nature proceeding from the Throne.

Remember, you can discern a false prophet because they are busy trying to steal the thunder from God and be the flashy lightning that draws attention to themselves. You will know the genuine prophet because they carry the authentic words, signs, and wonders that draw the attention to the Lord.

When we think of how powerful and brilliant the manifestations of God are, it makes us hungry to represent Him correctly. This means as genuine ministers, we must not be given to what marks a false prophet or immature prophetic minister by trying to portray ourselves as powerful thunder. In addition, we must not seek to be flashy or overly sensational in our actions or presentation. We must not try to create our own "earthquakes" and "shake" people falsely through manipulation. Instead, it must be by the genuine anointing of the Holy Spirit. God's voice as it proceeds from the Throne is powerful and thundering without our help, especially when it is released from pure vessels with pure motives. This will always move people with a deep impact and purpose like the shaking of an earthquake. It is to remind us what our prophetic voices, giftings, and callings are meant to do it in their purity and purpose. It is not trying to be powerful, appear powerful, steal the show, and shake people up for our own glory and benefit. Yet when God speaks from His heart and from the Throne Room, it will yield words that will cause men's bones to rattle!

I was once invited into the office of a nation's president to pray and minister to him. I didn't feel any earthshaking words and certainly wasn't going to act flashy like lightning or just be another in a number of voices that may have spoken to him already. I simply waited on the Lord to see what He would say and what He would want me to do. I began to minister a word to him. His response was surprising to me. He replied, "You have told me six things that I have not shared with anyone. I have sought psychics, priests, and others, but your words shook me." It was the first time I ever saw prophecy as something that shakes people. It is how I began to see the prophetic in conjunction with earthquakes. As Throne Room prophets and those who prophesy, we need to have a level of authority that people recognize as us speaking from the Lord and not just throwing out empty words. It is always a good reminder that we don't try to manufacture a powerful or thunderous delivery. Just allow God to manifest as He desires and it will bring honor to Him with earth-shaking results!

BEWARE OF FALSE "HORNED" PROPHETS AND THRONE ROOM COUNTERFEITS

I want to look at what I call "horned" prophets who are revealed as counterfeits in Scripture. We first need to understand that horns were used in the Bible as displays of power and authority. We see this with David, who proclaimed he would be anointed with a fresh horn of power. *"But my horn shalt thou exalt like the horn of an unicorn; I shall be anointed with fresh oil"* (Ps. 92:10). But not all horns are to God's glory and honor. For example, God declared the horns of the wicked would be cut off (see Ps. 75:10).

So what do we mean by "horned" prophets? These horns represent the behaviors and characteristics of false prophets who act and speak like they have thunderous power from the Lord. Mixed with their flashy displays of counterfeit lightning, they attempt to draw others to them and their voice. We will see this more clearly in a bit when we look at Zedekiah and how his dramatic performance revealed him to be a Throne Room counterfeit.

We must beware of these horned prophets, as it will help us accurately discern why they are false prophets! We find some of these Throne Room counterfeits in First Kings 22, when two kings—Jehoshaphat, the king of Judah, and King Ahab, who ruled over Israel—considered going to war with the king of Syria.

And the king of Israel said unto his servants, Know ye that Ramoth in Gilead is ours, and we be still, and take it not out of the hand of the king of Syria? (1 Kings 22:3)

They sought wisdom, guidance, and prophetic counsel as to whether they should go to war with the king of Syria. Before they considered engaging in this battle, they sought prophetic counsel from 400 prophets who served King Ahab.

Then the king of Israel gathered the prophets together, about four hundred men, and said unto them, Shall I go against Ramothgilead to battle, or shall I forbear? And they said, Go up; for the Lord shall deliver it into the hand of the king (1 Kings 22:6).

These 400 were on Ahab's payroll, you could say, and told the king what he would want to hear. Every one of them agreed that victory was the word from the Lord, and they unanimously prophesied they were to go to war. However, these prophetic words did not settle with the God-fearing king, Jehoshaphat. He insisted they inquire of a true prophet of the Lord.

And Jehoshaphat said, Is there not here a prophet of the Lord besides, that we might enquire of him? (1 Kings 22:7)

The person of choosing was Micaiah, a true prophet of the Lord. However, there was one problem—this prophet spoke true words that King Ahab didn't like. Micaiah was unlike the other 400 who told him what he wanted to hear.

> *And the king of Israel said unto Jehoshaphat, There is yet one man, Micaiah the son of Imlah, by whom we may enquire of the Lord: but I hate him; for he doth not prophesy good concerning me, but evil. And Jehoshaphat said, Let not the king say so. Then the king of Israel called an officer, and said, Hasten hither Micaiah the son of Imlah* (1 Kings 22:8-9).

Before Micaiah the prophet was to appear, the two kings, Jehoshaphat and Ahab, both sat on their thrones dressed in their robes as all the prophets prophesied before them. As this story continues, we see this horned prophet named Zedekiah, the head prophet, arise. He prophesies a false word to these two kings and puts on a thunderous, dramatic, flashy presentation in the king's throne room. It was a perverted and false presentation of the genuine we saw with the apostle John's experience.

> *And Zedekiah the son of Chenaanah made him horns of iron: and he said, Thus saith the Lord, With these shalt thou push the Syrians, until thou have consumed them* (1 Kings 22:11).

This thunderous and flashy display that Zedekiah puts on is what identifies him as a false prophet or horned prophet. It is not the presentation or even the prophetic act of the horns necessarily, because many prophets in Scripture were demonstrative and demonstrated prophetic acts with their prophecies. What Zedekiah displayed was his own false spirit needing recognition, and as a result he opened himself up and spoke under the influence of an evil spirit, which we will see as the story continues.

Notice the impressive, convincing display he used to mislead the king as a Throne Room counterfeit. False prophets often impress their listeners with their dramatic presentation, and people are often led to believe this proves their legitimacy. It was with this prideful display of iron horns, while seeming as if he was prophesying correctly, that opened him up to a lying spirit. Now again, this false horned prophet and the others were supposed to have been prophets who spoke on behalf of the Lord, but they were actually prophesying from a lying, demonic spirit. Zedekiah used these iron horns to appear thunderous in his powerful prophetic gift parading before the kings. He continued his flashy display before the kings, acting as a true prophet speaking on behalf of the Lord. Instead, he was misleading these two earthly kings, not as a genuine prophet but rather a flashy Throne Room counterfeit.

In the same way today, prophetic ministers must not misrepresent our Lord and King in their character, power, or words. These are marks of a false prophet. They want acclaim and recognition, so they act in an authoritative manner. There is nothing wrong with having true power and authority from the Lord, but it should point people's attention to the Lord and not ourselves.

We see another example of wicked horns in the apostle John's encounter regarding a beast that had seven horns.

And there appeared another wonder in heaven; and behold a great red dragon, having seven heads and ten horns, and seven crowns upon his heads. And his tail drew the third part of the stars of heaven, and did cast them to the earth: and the dragon stood before the woman which was ready to be delivered, for to devour her child as soon as it was born (Revelation 12:3-4).

The horns in these verses represent the flesh or what we refer to as horned prophets—those who minister not with the horn of Holy Spirit's power, authority, or accuracy but rather from their own flesh or a false spirit.

How is that these seven heads and ten horns represent flesh? The seven heads and ten horns add up to seventeen, which is the number of the flesh. In Galatians, we find seventeen acts described as the works of the flesh.

Now the works of the flesh are manifest, which are these; Adultery, fornication, uncleanness, lasciviousness, idolatry, witchcraft, hatred, variance, emulations, wrath, strife, seditions, heresies, envyings, murders, drunkenness, revellings, and such like: of the which I tell you before, as I have also told you in time past, that they which do such things shall not inherit the kingdom of God (Galatians 5:19-21).

These seventeen characteristics of the flesh are often the fleshly attributes and character of false prophets. They are not people of the spirit but of the flesh. We can also refer to the works of the flesh listed in Galatians as the seventeen "horns" of the flesh, marking the fruit of the false prophet or "horned" prophet.

While Zedekiah was acting in the flesh under an influence of an evil spirit, all the other prophets joined in with his thunderous, lightning presentation, prophesying falsely. They were all declaring the kings should go forward into battle with a victorious outcome!

> *And all the prophets prophesied so, saying, Go up to Ramothgilead, and prosper: for the Lord shall deliver it into the king's hand* (1 Kings 22:12).

All the prophets were declaring one thing, but now the moment would arise for a true prophet to speak on behalf of the Lord God Himself. Yet before Micaiah would prophesy the words of the Lord, he himself would be tested in his prophetic gifting and his character. Would he go with the word God had spoken and be the only one speaking something different, or would he sign on falsely with the others? Would he be swayed by the thunderous, flashy presentation of these false prophets, or would he remain true to his calling and to the Lord?

This is an area where prophets and people who prophesy must continually examine ourselves.

We must ensure our hearts are right and pure before the Lord and our desire to please Him is greater than our desire to please man.

For do I now persuade men, or God? or do I seek to please men? for if I yet pleased men, I should not be the servant of Christ (Galatians 1:10).

And the messenger that was gone to call Micaiah spake unto him, saying, Behold now, the words of the prophets declare good unto the king with one mouth: let thy word, I pray thee, be like the word of one of them, and speak that which is good (1 Kings 22:13).

Micaiah refused to give in to the popular trend and word for the day, and instead he spoke what the Lord had given him. This must be the standard of every prophetic minister as well and is what marks a genuine prophet from a false one. The true will always side with God and with truth, not being swayed by what man wants, like the false prophet does. This is especially true when the word you have been given isn't popular and appears false because the majority are saying something other than the word you have received from the Lord.

The mere fact that Micaiah would not compromise became his safeguard. It is what safeguards all who prophesy. This is what marked Micaiah as a true prophet who would speak on behalf of the Lord. He recognized that he was speaking on behalf of a higher kingdom than the one he was addressing. At first, he mocked these other prophets by appearing as though he agreed with them. He used this approach to reveal to the kings the difference between the word he would give and what the other 400 were prophesying.

> *So he came to the king. And the king said unto*
> *him, Micaiah, shall we go against Ramothgilead to*
> *battle, or shall we forbear? And he answered him,*
> *Go, and prosper: for the Lord shall deliver it into the*
> *hand of the king* (1 Kings 22:15).

Micaiah spoke this word to mock and expose the other false prophets and to establish that his words were different. He didn't need to draw attention to himself and create some thunderous moment to convince his hearers that he was speaking on behalf of the Lord. Instead, he did so with thunderous words of true authority and a display of lightning accuracy. His prophecy would reveal that God did not say these two kings were to go to war or even be victorious. In fact, he prophesied that if they did, the result would be death like sheep without their shepherd.

> *And he said, I saw all Israel scattered upon the hills,*
> *as sheep that have not a shepherd: and the Lord*
> *said, These have no master: let them return every*
> *man to his house in peace. And the king of Israel*
> *said unto Jehoshaphat, Did I not tell thee that he*
> *would prophesy no good concerning me, but evil?*
> (1 Kings 22:17)

Of course, Ahab did not like this prophecy, but it exposed the darkness and the sources from which the other 400 prophets were speaking and operating. Micaiah further revealed that all the other 400 prophets including Zedekiah were false. He revealed through a heavenly vision given him that a false and lying spirit was in the mouths of Zedekiah and the other prophets.

> *And he said, Hear thou therefore the word of the Lord: I saw the Lord sitting on his throne, and all the host of heaven standing by him on his right hand and on his left. And the Lord said, Who shall persuade Ahab, that he may go up and fall at Ramothgilead? And one said on this manner, and another said on that manner. And there came forth a spirit, and stood before the Lord, and said, I will persuade him. And the Lord said unto him, Wherewith? And he said, I will go forth, and I will be a lying spirit in the mouth of all his prophets. And he said, Thou shalt persuade him, and prevail also: go forth, and do so. Now therefore, behold, the Lord hath put a lying spirit in the mouth of all these thy prophets, and the Lord hath spoken evil concerning thee (1 Kings 22:19-23).*

He declared that he got this prophetic revelation from the Throne Room as a true prophet, and all the others received their revelations by the influence of a demonic, lying, and false spirit. He let the kings know that the other prophets were persuaded by this lying spirit.

As Micaiah exposed the others, the false prophet Zedekiah grew angry and struck him, the genuine prophetic voice. This is another behavior of false prophets today—they rise up and attack the true prophetic voices in much the same way Zedekiah slapped Micaiah in the face.

> *But Zedekiah the son of Chenaanah went near, and smote Micaiah on the cheek, and said, Which way went the Spirit of the Lord from me to speak unto thee?* (1 Kings 22:24)

The word translated "slapped" in this verse is the Hebrew word *nakah*. It means a "striking to cause a wound." This was not a nice slap in the face! The slap in this verse reveals the false spirit that attacks the genuine prophetic with the influence of witchcraft and evil spirits. It is meant to wound the true prophetic voice and force it into silence.

The prophecy that Micaiah delivers lands him in jail to silence him. This is always the goal of the false—especially evil spirits that operate through religious traditions, teachings, and doctrines. They stone them, or like with Micaiah, they "slap them in the face" by calling them names, casting their names out as evil, falsifying their words, and trying to silence them. Like Zedekiah, they try to convince others that the true prophets are actually false. Their intent is to wound them and their reputations.

Yet as in the case of Micaiah, true prophets and those who genuinely prophesy today have God as their defender. The key is to stay in love, forgiveness, kindness, and not to be afraid of being bold, continuing to speak as the Lord reveals. Do this with the right authority and reputable support system around you. Every prophetic voice must trust that the Lord will defend His gift in you and through you.

It is vital to understand the pure attributes of thunder, lightning, and voices that proceed from God's Throne so we can recognize the counterfeits! Ahab's false prophets appeared like they had been in the heavenly Throne Room and were speaking and ministering on behalf of the king. In reality, they were counterfeit, horned prophets, stealing the thunder as they tried to be the most powerful voice and the anointed star, flashing their supernatural feats.

We must not be deceived by their counterfeits, antics, words, and showboating. They are often outright sophisticated at what they do, appearing innocent and even trustworthy. They prophesy things that people want to hear.

How could these kings be misled by these false prophets? A helpful thing to consider is to look at how and what Jesus prophesied. His words were precise and specific. This should be what prophets and those who prophesy desire as well. When we give words from the Lord that are more precise and specific, they should carry what we find in Jesus' message in Matthew 24. It is a wonderful example of a clear, precise prophecy. He gave the *what, why, when* and then He gave *instructions.* He explained *what* would happen and *why.* Then He mentioned *when* in regard to the signs that would appear, and lastly He gave *instructions* and advice on what they should do in regard to the prophetic revelations and warnings.

Jesus was very clear about *what* would happen. The walls of the temple would be smashed and destroyed. This prophecy was fulfilled. Jesus explained clearly *why* these events would happen. When asked *when* these things would happen, He gave a very precise answer. They would not happen immediately, but they would come in the lifetime of most of the people listening. Jesus also gave a couple of *signs* that would show them *when* the time of action was close (Jerusalem surrounded by an army). This prophecy was fulfilled, too. Jesus also gave good prophetic *advice* about what people should do when the troubles started. They should flee to the mountains. Those who heeded this warning were kept safe.

This prophecy gave direction, it had weight to it, and was precise and not vague. Remember, God always has a redemptive plan, especially in prophetic warnings. As we mentioned previously, He will always offer a plan of hope and a plan of help if the people will heed the word of warning. It is important that we know and understand this when we hear prophets warn of future disastrous events, which many do. However, very few are explaining what God is doing and how He will work through these events to bring change. It's important we don't leave out God's plan of hope when we prophesy.

A problem that arises today is that there are some who seem to enjoy giving warnings of judgment on the world, but they are less enthusiastic about strategies that would require them to take action to bring in the victory of God. We must not get caught up with prophesying what is popular or speak words out of fear or our own biases. This is where prophets can become false, as they prophesy what is obvious or what is according to what man wants and says. They spend more time repeating what is on the news or what is being predominantly spoken through the media or by the majority of people like the 400 false prophets did.

IDENTIFYING FALSE, HORNED PROPHETS

Jesus mentioned that we should know people but especially false prophets by their fruits or characteristics (see Matt. 7:15-16). We have to be discerning and know what these fruits are, because false prophets appear to be genuinely from God. We've discussed the works of the flesh listed in Galatians, but there are some other characteristics we should be aware of when seeking to discern false prophets, and they're not always so obvious.

When the apostle John sees a heavenly vision of what looks like an innocent lamb with horns, it opens its mouth and speaks as a dragon. This is a great picture of the false, horned prophet—those who look innocent but are actually wolves in sheep's clothing.

> *And I beheld another beast coming up out of the earth; and he had two horns like a lamb, and he spake as a dragon* (Revelation 13:11).

John saw a lamb with horns who spoke as a dragon! In other words, the false horned prophets look innocent and appear to be from the Lord, but when they open their mouths they speak from a false spirit. It is vital that we know that false prophets can often appear and sound like they are Christian, genuine, and speaking from Heaven. Not everything that appears genuine is such, and just because a word has a "thus saith the Lord" on it does not mean it is from Heaven! In addition, false prophets often appear as the lamb that John saw—innocent or speaking on behalf of the Lamb Himself, but they are not. This is why we must consider more than just their words.

Let's look at ten attitudes, behaviors, and fruits that will help us recognize those who appear genuine but who are indeed false. Remember, they seek to steal the thunder and "wow" you with lightning-like displays of power in order to draw you into their deception.

1. Prediction

False prophets fall into predicting rather than prophesying words with a promise. A person who spends time always trying to predict something will fall into tapping into the wrong source and feeling the need to perform. Again, this is because many audiences actually crave prediction about the future. If a prophetic vessel gives in to that demand, they will start performing for their hearers by predicting future events rather than prophesying God's purposes. Anytime we fall into the pressure of prophesying to fulfil the demands of our audience, we will start doing what makes us feel powerful rather than operating in genuine anointing. This is why the Bible says that He gives His secrets to His *servants* the prophets (see Amos 3:7). Prophets are to foretell or declare the future—not based on chance, guesses, or predictions but through sharing God's heart as His servants.

2. Performance

Horned prophets give the people what they want to hear; thus, they perform rather than being under divine inspiration. Jesus had to address this when He spoke to the people about the prophet John the Baptist, because they wanted him to perform: "What did you come out to see?" (see Matt. 11:9). It is important that we don't let men dictate when we speak but we call upon the Holy Spirit and obey what He wants said. Watch out for "showboat" prophets! They resort more to sensationalism rather than the supernatural!

3. *Pride*

False prophets strive to be heard and they love to be seen. They look for ways to be elevated and considered powerful. Remember, this is why Zedekiah the prophet displayed the horns when he was speaking to the kings. He was trying to prove that he and his prophecy were powerful. The problem was that he misled Ahab and was wrong.

Humility is key. Jesus is our best example of prophetic humility, and humility is a necessity for every believer and prophetic minister. In Luke 14:7-10, Jesus noticed how the guests picked the places of honor at the table. He began to explain that when someone invites you to a wedding feast, you shouldn't assume the place of honor at the table. This is because a person more distinguished than you may have also been invited and the host may come and say to you, "Give this person your seat." Then, in humiliation, you will be moved to the least important place. Instead, when you are invited, take the lowest place so that when your host comes, he will say to you, "Friend, move up to a better place." Then you will be honored in the presence of all the other guests.

Horned prophets and immature prophetic people will often attempt to find the highest place at gatherings and seek the highest platforms to promote their words and ministry. If we fall into this trap, we run the risk of not speaking under the divine inspiration of the Holy Spirit but from a spirit of pride. Psalm 5:5 tells us, *"The arrogant cannot stand in your presence"* (NIV). This is exactly opposite of the true Spirit of prophecy (see Rev. 19:10). Prophecy is meant to testify to the awesomeness of Jesus, not to the awesomeness of ourselves.

4. *Harshness, Bad News, and Warnings*

False, horned prophets always feel the need to come up with a predictive word of judgment, doom and gloom, tragedy, or catastrophe in order to prove the legitimacy of their calling and prophecies. As we discussed previously, it's not hard to look around at the world and see the bad things happening and then attach a "prophetic word" to it. The truth is, it takes more faith and anointing to prophesy good, especially in dark times. For example, Jesus said in Luke 4:18 that He was anointed to preach good news. He announced this during a very dark time in history. So we need to stretch our eyes and ears to come up higher and prophesy good in evil times, light in darkness, truth amidst error!

At the same time, we can learn from the prophets in Scripture how to deliver words of admonishment and warning effectively, when needed. Consider the prophet Nathan and how he told a story to get David's attention in order to share a very admonishing word concerning David's adultery with Bathsheba. He told it in a way that drew David into sympathy for the victim, who was actually David's own victim! As a result, it was very difficult for David to reject the bad news (see 2 Sam. 12:1-7). Also, the prophet Jeremiah used many symbolic examples and objects to bring warnings and also to give hope. This drew people in and opened their hearts to the word (see Jer. 13:1-12). We need to be wise and not harsh in how we deliver our words. It's important to share the Lord's words with taste and grace. When we don't, we run the risk of causing others to not trust the Lord's heart toward them.

5. They prophesy from the wrong source and wrong spirit.

False, horned prophets receive and deliver information from the source of fear, a spirit of darkness, and even witchcraft. Remember the lamb with horns that spoke like a dragon in Revelation 13:11. What we feed on or align ourselves with determines not only our mindsets and perspectives, but the spirit that influences us and our words. Is it the Holy Spirit of God or a contrary, evil spirit?

6. They are accountable to no one or only those who agree with them.

Do you remember how Jesus' first miracle was submitted to the governor of the feast (see John 2)? He showed His submission by having the governor do a taste test of the water that He'd turned into wine. Again, pride can easily arise when one is extremely gifted but underdeveloped. Proper accountability helps a person stay humble because they are able to receive feedback as well as balanced training.

7. *They prophesy from their own heart, soul, emotions, or opinions.*

The key to being a genuine prophetic vessel who operates at a higher level is having the ability to communicate God's heart effectively. False prophets are not concerned about the Lord's heart. Always remember that when God's heart is prioritized and not ignored, it acts as a protection. Learn to hate what God hates, love what He loves, and find out His feelings on a matter. God's heart can be grieved, and we must always consider how He feels in every situation. Genesis 6:6 says that God's heart was grieved, or His heart was broken. We must have the right spirit and attitude in our message and delivery and not be like Jonah, who paid more attention to his own cultural bias against the Ninevites than to the word of the Lord.

8. *They prophesy according to trends and what is popular.*

False prophets can often be found taking information from news headlines or the discussion of the day and presenting it as the word of the Lord. For example, people sometimes make it seem as though whatever direction the culture is going is the will of God and what we are to follow. The problem most times is that, though these leadings are supported in culture, they're actually contradictory to Scripture. Information and leading from popular trends often carry a contrary spirit rather than truth. This can look like fear or compromise. In most cases, biblical prophets carried words that were contrary to the direction *society* was going. The popular word among people is not always what is popular in Heaven.

9. *They concentrate more on their gift than the manifestation of the Spirit.*

False or horned prophets concentrate on their gift or on themselves rather than depending or focusing on the Holy Spirit. Serving the Lord and ministering to others is never about us showboating, drawing attention to our gift, calling, anointing, or ministry. Our focus must always be upon the Lord, as He deserves all the credit and glory.

10. *They act carelessly and display acts of immaturity that prey on others.*

Those who act in these manners often come against the mature Throne Room prophets, especially true prophets who disagree with them, their character, methods, or prophecies. *"But Zedekiah the son of Chenaanah went near, and smote Micaiah on the cheek"* (1 Kings 22:24). Remember, this striking at or against Micaiah, a true Throne Room prophet, revealed Zedekiah's immaturity and false spirit.

Understanding all of these attributes will help us to identify the horns of deceit and falsehood. We must remember that prophets can often start off right but ignore the genuine marks and traits and begin to accept wrong practices and behaviors, which quickly will cause them to become false.

FALSE PROPHETS AND TEACHERS

It is important to note that the concept of "false" is one that the Lord takes very seriously, and Scripture is clear on warnings against both prophesying and teaching falsely. Though we are discussing prophets, it is worth mentioning that the New Testament actually mentions false teachers more than false prophets. This is because false teachers generally had a wide influence, and they were teaching false doctrines of Scripture that could easily move someone away from the true Gospel and into heresy. In the case of both the prophet and the teacher, it was their bad conduct and character that classified them as false. Remember, Jesus said we would know them by their fruit—their lifestyle, character, and conduct.

Let's look at some things that false prophets are not or that they do not do:

- False prophets are not willing to be led by the Holy Spirit.

Finally, a spirit came forward, stood before the Lord and said, "I will entice him." "By what means?" the Lord asked. "I will go out and be a deceiving spirit in the mouths of all his prophets," he said. "You will succeed in enticing him," said the Lord. "Go and do it" (1 Kings 22:21-25 NIV).

- False prophets do not have the true word of God in them.

They have lied about the Lord; they said, "He will do nothing! No harm will come to us; we will never see sword or famine. The prophets are but wind and the word is not in them; so let what they say be done to them" (Jeremiah 5:12-13 NIV).

- False prophets have no shame.

"From the least to the greatest, all are greedy for gain; prophets and priests alike, all practice deceit. They dress the wound of my people as though it were not serious. 'Peace, peace,' they say, when there is no peace. Are they ashamed of their detestable conduct? No, they have no shame at all; they do not even know how to blush. So they will fall among the fallen; they will be brought down when I punish them," says the Lord (Jeremiah 6:13-15 NIV).

- False prophets are not appointed by the Lord.

The prophets are prophesying lies in my name. I have not sent them or appointed them or spoken to them. They are prophesying to you false visions, divinations, idolatries and the delusions of their own minds. Therefore this is what the Lord says about the prophets who are prophesying in my name: I did not send them (Jeremiah 14:14-15 NIV).

- False prophets do not offer true hope.

This is what the Lord Almighty says: "Do not listen to what the prophets are prophesying to you; they fill you with false hopes. They speak visions from their own minds, not from the mouth of the Lord" (Jeremiah 23:16 NIV).

- False prophets are not speaking the Lord's words.

Their visions are false and their divinations a lie. Even though the Lord has not sent them, they say,

"The Lord declares," and expect him to fulfill their words. Have you not seen false visions and uttered lying divinations when you say, "The Lord declares," though I have not spoken? (Ezekiel 13:6-7 NIV)

- False prophets do not benefit others.

"I am against the prophets who steal from one another words supposedly from me. Yes," declares the Lord, "I am against the prophets who wag their own tongues and yet declare, 'The Lord declares.' Indeed, I am against those who prophesy false dreams," declares the Lord. "They tell them and lead my people astray with their reckless lies, yet I did not send or appoint them. They do not benefit these people in the least," declares the Lord (Jeremiah 23:28-32 NIV).

Second Peter 2 further describes false prophets and teachers:

- False prophets bring in damnable heresies, messages, and teachings (verse 1).
- They deny the Lord (verse 1).
- They are covetous, and their words make merchandise of people (verse 3).
- They walk in the flesh (verse 10).
- False prophets despise authority (verse 10).
- They are presumptuous and not Holy Spirit led (verse 10).
- They speak evil of dignitaries (verse 10).

- They are immoral, and their eyes are full of adultery (verse 14).
- They can't cease from sin (verse 14).
- They go after unstable or young Christians and people (verse 14).
- They go the way of Balaam, using witchcraft and compromise (verse 15).
- They speak swelling, convincing words meant to deceive (verse 18).
- They are corrupt (verse 19).

As we've previously discussed, it's the discipline of staying in the Lord's presence and close to His heart that keeps genuine prophetic vessels from going down the wrong path.

KNOWING WHEN TO RELEASE A WORD

As we bring this chapter to a close, let's look at the Throne Room prophet's discipline regarding when and how they release words they receive. This discipline is another distinct difference between a horned prophet and a Throne Room prophet. The horned prophet's pride, performance, and need for power is completely opposite of that of the true prophet. Because the false, horned prophet's motive is to be seen, heard, and recognized, they do not discipline themselves in character, behavior, or delivery of their "prophetic" revelation. On the other hand, the Throne Room prophet is more cautious, considerate, and has the fear of the Lord that acts as a safeguard.

This person exhibits a life that strives for purity and holiness, and it is evident through their strong character, conviction, and desire to partner with the Spirit of Truth. That takes discipline on all fronts. It is why true prophetic vessels will carry a greater glory or weight upon them than the false, horned prophet. True Throne Room prophets understand the weight of responsibility with which they have been entrusted; they honor the sacred heart of the Lord and what He chooses to reveal. They are disciplined in waiting on the Lord and waiting to share the words they have been given. This is what the Scripture means when it references prophets who were to hold on to the word of the Lord, meaning to wait *for* and *on* the Lord (see 2 Kings 4:29 NLT). This requires discipline and maturity.

As those who covet Throne Room prophecy, we must learn the difference between speaking a word the moment we receive it and waiting to speak a word later on. The Holy Spirit will sometimes have us speak a spontaneous word, but we must be sensitive and willing to wait if the Spirit is telling us to do so. In waiting, we speak later—not because we are in fear, but because we must allow the prophetic word to be strongly deposited in us. There is nothing in Scripture that says a spontaneous prophecy is superior to one that is pondered for a time and edited to sharpen its delivery. Remember, the Lord is free to choose how He will operate in any situation. We must be led of the Spirit and tapped into the Spirit as manner of lifestyle. This way, we will know when to wait and will be ready in season and out of season to deliver a pure, pinpointed, and accurate prophecy.

There are times God wants us to speak right now at a specific time and holding back is not what the Lord wants us to do. However, there are other times a prophetic word requires we wait and let the word build in us so we minister it in the right spirit, clarity, and accuracy. The Lord often shakes us out of our comfort zones. He will sometimes be spontaneous when we want to be cautious or wait. Then at other times, God will want us to wait when we want to be spontaneous and speak a word right now. The benefit of a spontaneous word is that the Holy Spirit can drop it into our hearts unexpectedly, before our minds get going and our flesh has a chance to get in the way.

When we have received a word from the Lord, the first thing we should do is ask Him what He wants us to do with it. We should not assume that He wants us to speak it out. This is where false prophets ignore true prophetic protocol. Remember, they speak without waiting as they live to "wow" you in the moment with their sensationalism!

Always remember when ministering in the prophetic that the Lord may want us to sit on a prophecy and wait and pray. This will build maturity in us and sharpen our gifting. At other times we need to be prayed up, full of His Word and Spirit, and be ready if He nudges us to deliver a word *now*. Whether it is a word to be released immediately or a word we should hold on to for some time, we should always ask Him for interpretation and guidance to deliver it. This can be done at the moment the word of the Lord comes. Never forget that many true words are spoiled because they are incorrectly handled or not given in the right timing. Some words are meant for us to ponder and wait to deliver, and others are meant to share in the present moment. A good way to know is, you will feel prompted by a strong feeling and unction from the Holy Spirit to deliver it now, and if you don't, you will be disobeying the Lord. At other times, a strong feeling or caution will be given inside your heart that prompts you, restrains you, and even commands you to wait and pray the word through before sharing. The key is to strive to recognize the heavenly flow that proceeds from the Throne and to stay connected to heart of God at all times. Whether the Lord instructs you to prophesy in the moment or to wait, you will know and you will grow!

We've seen how Scripture describes false prophets and those who are not truly seeking the Lord's heart in their message and ministry. Unfortunately, tremendous damage has been done to people in the name of "prophecy," which has actually not come from the Lord but from fleshly desires or the influence of evil spirits. As those who seek to represent the Lord well in prophetic ministry, we can raise the standard of the prophetic in our day by walking in integrity and holiness.

Let's make it our goal to be the thunderous voice of the Lord with compassion and authority, at His leading alone. Let's pray and believe that we will, with lightning-like precision and power, present ourselves, our words, and displays of supernatural manifestations bearing witness to His voice. As it was with the apostle John and those who met God at Mount Sinai, we will experience the pure, mighty presence of His Spirit that will move both us and others. May the genuine prophetic flow powerfully through us as it proceeds from His Throne!

Chapter Seven

REPRESENTING THE THRONE ROOM

> *"And in the midst of the throne, and round about the throne, were four beasts full of eyes before and behind. And the first beast was like a lion, and the second beast like a calf, and the third beast had a face as a man, and the fourth beast was like a flying eagle. And the four beasts had each of them six wings about him; and they were full of eyes within: and they rest not day and night, saying, Holy, holy, holy, Lord God Almighty, which was, and is, and is to come."*
> —REVELATION 4:6-8

I want to consider one final aspect of John's Throne Room revelation that I believe will encourage us. The appearance of the four beasts around the Throne give us insight into what we are called to as representatives of the Throne Room. These four

creatures were full of eyes that appeared as a lion, a calf, a face of a man, and lastly as a flying eagle. What did these represent and how do they apply to us today?

These four beasts reveal important truths that are to be applied today. Knowing what these faces represent will help us come up higher in our walk with God and also our prophetic giftings. As we look at these four beasts, our Throne Room representations or images, we will get a good idea of what authentic prophetic vessels must look like in order to be easily recognized by others. When we bear these images, or faces, it will help to discern the authentic from the immature or even the false. You might be asking, "What are the prophetic applications of these four beasts?" Let's look at them in the order they're listed in Scripture.

THE FOUR FACES

First, the lion represents our authority given by God to rule and reign with Him. To the prophet, it also represents the authority we were given when we were chosen and established by God (see Eph. 4:11). Remember, God sets these gifts and manifestations into His Church for those in His Kingdom and the earth as it pleases Him. The face of the lion reminds us of the positional authority that is delegated to us and not self-appointed. When we are submitted to the Lord and appointed by Him, we then carry the boldness to speak His words like a lion. *"The wicked flee when no man pursueth: but the righteous are bold as a lion"* (Prov. 28:1). Not only will we step into a boldness to speak His words, but the word of the Lord will be in our mouths with power and authority. We will release His prophetic words and sounds like a lion roaring through us as we prophesy! *"The lion hath roared, who will not fear? the Lord God hath spoken, who can but prophesy?"* (Amos 3:8).

The face of the lion also reminds us of the position and attitude we must take when we are faced with opposition from others as well as the demonic realm. As prophetic vessels, we have to learn, especially when some may oppose what we prophesy, to stay in love and keep speaking boldly when attacked by those who oppose the genuine words of the Lord. The face of a lion is to remind us that demonic forces do not like those who speak for God and reveal His secrets. We must have our faces like a lion, meaning confident and bold, and we must never back down from the enemy. King David's mighty men were described as having faces of lions, speaking of their warrior attributes and Throne Room representation of the king they served.

> *And of the Gadites there separated themselves unto David into the hold to the wilderness men of might, and men of war fit for the battle, that could handle shield and buckler, whose faces were like the faces of lions, and were as swift as the roes upon the mountains* (1 Chronicles 12:8).

Second, John sees the face of an ox. What does this represent prophetically? An ox is one who is willing to do the work, bear the burdens, and even to sacrifice himself in laboring for others. This face of the ox shows us that we are to exhibit the heart and lifestyle of a servant in our giftings and callings.

This is especially true for those called to the prophetic office; our gifting is meant to serve the Lord as His voice and be available as a service to His people. The face of a true prophetic vessel should always be one of humility and Christlike character of service. This is another telltale sign of a false prophet: they do not exhibit humility, and rather than taking on the face of a servant, they glory in being served.

In Scripture, oxen represent serving, as we see when Elisha was plowing with twelve yoke of oxen upon meeting Elijah.

> *So he departed thence, and found Elisha the son of Shaphat, who was plowing with twelve yoke of oxen before him, and he with the twelfth: and Elijah passed by him, and cast his mantle upon him* (1 Kings 19:19).

Taking on the face of the ox, or serving, is not always glamorous, and the ones serving can often be overlooked. Yet it is the mature prophetic vessels who put more emphasis on being a servant of the Lord and being a servant to others. They don't seek recognition or have a need to be in the spotlight. They are content and secure enough in who they are and their gifting to make sure the Lord is glorified, and they serve others to help them reach their destinies and callings. One such example is found in the story of David and Goliath. There were two who helped David defeat Goliath who are not usually mentioned when we tell the story. Yet these two, prophetically speaking, took upon themselves the face of the ox that released David to carry out his gifting and calling, and they didn't need credit or recognition. Who were they? The Scripture tells us that in order for David to go to the front line to face Goliath he would have to leave his father's sheep with the sheep keeper and he would also need a baggage carrier.

> *And David rose up early in the morning, and left the sheep with a keeper, and took, and went, as Jesse had commanded him; and he came to the trench, as the host was going forth to the fight, and shouted for the battle. For Israel and the Philistines had put the battle in array, army against army. And David left his carriage in the hand of the keeper of the carriage, and ran into the army, and came and saluted his brethren (1 Samuel 17:20-22).*

These two who took on the face of the ox through serving were necessary to release and aid David in the gifting the Lord gave him. In the same way, we will be a blessing to others when we have the mindset of a servant.

Jesus spoke of the greatest in the Kingdom as the one who serves. He also took the form of a servant, or the face of a servant, through His humility and actions toward others and before His heavenly Father.

> *But made himself of no reputation, and took upon him the form of a servant, and was made in the likeness of men: and being found in fashion as a man, he humbled himself, and became obedient unto death, even the death of the cross (Philippians 2:7-8).*

The face of the ox also speaks the strength and energy we need in laboring for the Lord. As Throne Room representatives, we must be humble servants, willing to submit our giftings to the Lord and for ministering to the people. It also prophetically speaks of laboring in our giftings, ministries, and sharing the Gospel. Though prophetic gifting is important and necessary, God's heart is always toward the lost, and we must never forget that our primary call is to share His plan of salvation.

Third, John sees one of the four beasts as having the face of a man. This prophetically speaks of our face or identity as others look at us, our giftings, and ministries. We need to remember to keep it real, as people see our humanity or lives outside of our anointings or giftings. Jesus was the perfect example of this, being used powerfully in signs, wonders, and miracles but then also showing the face of a man when not performing miracles, like reclining at a table enjoying life with others without compromising.

The face of the man is represented in our character, conduct, integrity, and ministries as human vessels of the Lord. This should be seen in our morals, message, ministries, marriages, money matters, and integrity, to name a few. It is what marks the genuine prophetic vessel as they represent themselves genuinely to others in matters of everyday life. They aren't out to impress others and they don't live a double standard that leads to sin and compromise. Instead, they can flow powerfully in prophecy, the anointing, and the giftings the Lord has given them while maintaining a proper image of being real and genuine without any pretense. The face of the man is about the person who represents the Throne Room, not about the title or gift we have been given. It also speaks of the mature believer who develops in both their humanity and their giftings.

Finally, the eagle is representative of our seeing, hearing, and perceiving correctly from the Throne Room. Eagles operate from the high places, or in our case, the Throne Room. The prophets in Scripture were seen coming from the high places, which speaks of a spiritual position and the place of the spirit. They were returning from spending time with the Lord and with a prophetic company and were prophesying as a result of what they experienced in that place.

> *Thou shalt meet a company of prophets coming down from the high place with a psaltery, and a tabret, and a pipe, and a harp, before them; and they shall prophesy* (1 Samuel 10:5).

This high place where eagles soar is to be a continual reminder that your gift, anointing, and function will soar when you maintain a life of coming up higher and dwelling in the Throne Room! The face of the eagle also represents how we must watch and pray with prophetic eyes and keen prophetic awareness. Eagles have very keen eyesight, and this speaks of the relationship with the prophetic when prophets are called seers, given to visions, dreams, and prophetic insights. *"Let's go to the seer"* (1 Sam. 9:9). Eagles see better when they are in the sky and not as well on the ground. The same is true for every prophetic vessel—we will operate better in our giftings and callings when are spending time with the Lord and getting revelation from the heavenly realm. When we make it a habit to dwell in the high place of the Throne Room, we will be able to effectively minister to those in the earth as a true prophetic eagle.

As we can see, these four images that John saw give us a clear picture of how we should function and what we are to emulate. If you find these four characteristics in a prophetic vessel, you've found someone you can follow and trust. These are the genuine prophetic representations of the authentic prophetic minister and what false prophets pervert.

The false prophet takes on their own authority and will often sound powerful like a lion but are not roaring with the true prophetic sound from God. They want others to serve them like a yoke of oxen under their control and manipulation. In addition, they have a perverted, non-touchable presentation of themselves as a person, glorying in their own image and lacking genuine manners, authenticity, and purity of character. Lastly, the places they tap into are not the high place of the Throne Room but the high places of the occult realm, where their influence and revelation come from demonic sources.

It is interesting to note that John observed another unique quality of these four beasts that speaks to us prophetically. He saw that each of the beasts had six wings about them and they were full of eyes within.

> *And the four beasts had each of them six wings about him; and they were full of eyes within: and they rest not day and night, saying, Holy, holy, holy, Lord God Almighty, which was, and is, and is to come* (Revelation 4:8).

These six wings speak of their mobility or movement in the spirit. This is another quality found in a true prophetic vessel. True prophetic vessels know how to operate and move in the spirit realm as if they have wings, under the direction of the Lord they know and serve. It was with each movement of these beasts' wings that their eyes also moved, representing to us prophetic revelations, insights, and perspectives. When we begin to move in the anointing or our gifting, it must be with the Spirit's presence, which will give us better prophetic vision and accuracy.

This is an important necessity and discipline for the Throne Room prophet and for those who prophesy. If the Lord doesn't want any movement—meaning speaking, revealing, repeating, or manifesting something that He shows us in the Throne Room—then neither should we. We must not be too quick to share a specific word or to try to share a word before anyone else in order to receive the notoriety and credit for it. It is far better to understand how to move with the Spirit, like these four beasts and like the disciples.

> *And they went forth, and preached every where, the Lord working with them, and confirming the word with signs following. Amen* (Mark 16:20).

THE TWENTY-FOUR ELDERS AND THE THRONE ROOM PROPHET

> *And round about the throne were four and twenty seats: and upon the seats I saw four and twenty elders sitting, clothed in white raiment; and they had on their heads crowns of gold* (Revelation 4:4).

The apostle John was in the presence of the Lord Jesus Christ and the twenty-four elders of the Lamb. These elders were part of the leadership of the Throne Room. The prophetic application is no matter what our function, title, or how strong the manifestation of God is through us, we need to be submitted to the Lord and to godly counsel. We must never underestimate the importance of having the proper spiritual oversight, mentoring, and accountability of our lives and prophetic giftings. John saw that wisdom in the elders. For us, it is being accountable to those in healthy spiritual authority. This is what keeps Throne Room prophecy accurate and powerful! John also tells us what the elders were wearing.

> *And round about the throne were four and twenty seats: and upon the seats I saw four and twenty elders sitting, clothed in white raiment; and they had on their heads crowns of gold* (Revelation 4:4).

Did you notice that John mentions the white raiment before the crowns of gold upon their heads? The white raiment represents our character, our morals, and our pure lifestyle. This quality of holiness must always precede our giftings and callings.

To get a better picture of what this means to us as we seek to represent the Throne Room well, let's look at Acts 21:9. This verse speaks of Philip the evangelist having four virgin daughters who prophesied. *"And the same man had four daughters, virgins, which did prophesy"* (Acts 21:9). The descriptions of Philip's daughters and the twenty-four elders show us a prophetic parallel of divine order. Philip's daughters are mentioned first, followed by their virginity, and finally their prophetic giftings.

In the same way, the elders are mentioned first, then their white raiment (purity), followed by the crowns (giftings) upon their heads. Let's look at this more carefully.

The fact that these daughters are mentioned specifically as Philip's daughters is important. It shows us their relationship to their father and lets us know they were operating within his house and under his care and authority. Look again at the twenty-four elders. Where do we find them? They are in the presence of the Father, operating within His "house," the Throne Room, and under His care and authority. As prophetic people, we must display this same divine order. The four daughters and the twenty-four elders did not function in their anointing and giftings apart from their father's house, which for us speaks of a good local church, covering, and accountability.

The divine order continues as Scripture tells us that Philip's daughters were virgins. This speaks of purity and holiness. We see it in the elders as they were dressed in white raiment. Both examples show us the prophetic standard that we are to have as prophetic vessels. We, too, must maintain pure motives and prophecies. This purity precedes our prophetic gifting or operating in the office of the prophet, should we be called to it. We must always wear "garments" of pure and undefiled lives, honoring our heavenly Father as representatives of His Throne Room!

I want to touch on one more aspect of how the twenty-four elders were clothed. Scripture tells us their heads were crowned with gold, which represents the authority from which we minister in our giftings or offices. The crowns are mentioned *after* the white raiment, again showing us that purity must always precede our authority. In other words, personal purity and holiness must be our foundation, our standard, our code of moral conduct and ministry before we even mention that we prophesy or are called to a fivefold ministry office.

This is a key element in identifying false prophets. They will violate the principles of purity through pride, immorality, mishandling of money, mishandling their gifting, and mishandling people. False prophets focus on being powerfully crowned with authority while their garments (lifestyles) have been defiled. This is why a person can be anointed and, at the same time, shamelessly working iniquity according to Jesus. This doesn't grant permission, but often explains why some ministers who have lived an unrepentant lifestyle of moral corruption have continued to be used by God for a season. Eventually, it is revealed publicly that the person was living a lifestyle contrary to moral purity and integrity. How can that be?

God gives anointing based on our callings or our "job descriptions." A person's level of anointing is not necessarily God's endorsement or approval of their lifestyle. This is what Jesus was referring to in Matthew 7:22-23:

> *Many will say to me in that day, Lord, Lord, have we not prophesied in thy name? and in thy name*

*have cast out devils? and in thy name done many
wonderful works? And then will I profess unto them,
I never knew you: depart from me, ye that work
iniquity.*

These people were anointed, they had giftings and powerful manifestations, yet they were working iniquity. They
focused more on their crowns of authority than they did on
their garments of white. In order to minister rightly as pure
and holy Throne Room representatives, we must have a healthy
balance of both purity and authority.

Ecclesiastes 8 tells us to always keep our garments white
and our heads lacking no anointing. How do we wear this
white raiment today? We keep our garments white every time
we uphold a standard of holiness, purity, and honor toward
God, ourselves, and others. This standard should be seen in
everything we have been entrusted with in this life. Keeping
your garments white with a pure lifestyle that is pleasing to
God and recognizable to men will enhance your accuracy, gifting, and authority as you minister in the glorious anointing He
has placed upon you!

Honor must be found in our hearts and is also the garment
we wear. One cannot exhibit honor if it is not in their heart.
Just how important are these garments of holiness, purity,
integrity, and honor? We can find the answer by looking at our
Lord Jesus. He consistently displayed holiness, purity, integrity,
and honor. And as a man of honor, when He looked for someone to entrust with the sacred things of His heart, He chose
those who exhibited the same characteristics. Think about

it—to whom did He entrust His mother while hanging on the Cross? He entrusted His mother to John the beloved, who remained at Jesus' side, honoring Him while the others fled. Think for a moment how that applies to us today as we represent Him. If we want to be entrusted with something dear to the Lord's heart, like prophecy or His secrets, then we must have the same integrity and honor that John did.

Also, think about to whom Jesus entrusted His body—He left His body to Joseph of Arimathea, an honorable man. As we desire to reflect the Lord and flow in the secrets of His heart toward His Body (and the world), we must be like Joseph of Arimathea, willing to honor and care for the Lord's Body. This includes our brothers and sisters in the Lord, our local church, and His Church throughout the earth. We must be Throne Room representatives who forgive all and are kind to all. We must stay in a place of love and avoid rudeness, strife, gossip, and inappropriate conduct that would hurt the Lord and the Body of Christ! How we treat His Body is a telling sign of the degree of holiness and honor inside us.

Lastly, to whom did the Lord Jesus entrust His precious Spirit? It was entrusted to those who honored His words to tarry in Jerusalem until they'd been endued with power from on high. They were obedient in the upper room and were hungering for His presence, while they stayed consistent in prayer for His outpouring. We also see this honor in the first example of the Holy Spirit being poured out to the Gentiles at the house of Cornelius. What made this special? Once again, we find it had to do with honor. Cornelius was a devout or honorable man toward his house and toward the Lord. In the same way, when we keep our garments white with purity, holiness, and honor, then we will be entrusted with the power and person of the Holy Spirit in a more personal and demonstrated way, like the 120 who gathered in the upper room and those at Cornelius' house.

Again, we must remember that our garments are to always be white and our heads are to lack no anointing. If we want the anointing or the power of His Spirit displayed through us, then we must continually exhibit purity and integrity through our daily decisions, speech, and conduct. Those who spend more time focusing on their prophecies, ministries, or giftings more than on their garments will pollute the pure stream of the Lord's words and power.

Being entrusted with prophetic words from the Throne of God requires a life of no compromise and a protecting of our ears. For example, in the book of Jeremiah they were told to circumcise their ears, meaning that they were to cut away the flesh from their hearing (see Jer. 6:10). Jesus even spoke about intentionally cutting things off in our lives (see Matt. 5:29-30). He spoke of our eyes, which refer to prophetic revelation that comes from the Lord through visions, dreams, or anything that He is showing us. He also spoke of our hands, or things we choose to touch or align ourselves with, that can hinder the Lord's prophetic flow and cause us to tap into the wrong or even the false. He is stressing the importance of getting anything out of our lives that would cause us to stumble. Remember Philip's daughters—their lives and giftings were not compromised; as their lives were pure, so would be their prophecies and their stewarding of their gift before the Lord.

As we mentioned, John also saw the crowns of gold upon the elders' heads.

> *And round about the throne were four and twenty seats: and upon the seats I saw four and twenty elders sitting, clothed in white raiment; and they had on their heads crowns of gold* (Revelation 4:4).

These crowns speak of authority that has been delegated by our King, Jesus, whom we must represent well.

The crowns of gold upon their heads also signify another important aspect of honor—the crowns we have been given are for His honor, not our own. Notice what happens with these twenty-four elders when they put their true focus and attention on the Lord. They cast off their crowns and lay them before the King!

> *The four and twenty elders fall down before him that sat on the throne, and worship him that liveth for ever and ever, and cast their crowns before the throne, saying, Thou art worthy, O Lord, to receive glory and honour and power: for thou hast created all things, and for thy pleasure they are and were created* (Revelation 4:10-11).

This is a great reminder that the authority delegated to us is not for our own vainglory, but for His glory. We exist because of Him alone, and everything He does through our ministries is to honor Him and not ourselves. The crowns are for *His* honor and *His* glory!

The crowns we've been given also remind us that if we have been entrusted with a spiritual office by Jesus, we must always seek to stay within that office. We know the Lord has truly set us in a spiritual office when it has been confirmed by trusted leadership within His Body, with good fruit witnessed by others. In other words, if you are an evangelist, don't try to be a pastor; or if you are a pastor, don't seek to be a prophet; and so on.

It is also important that when we are called to a particular office, we stay within our given spiritual and positional authority. What do I mean by this? Within every office, there is a variety of spheres of influence and calling the Lord has appointed. For example, not every person who has been called as a prophet will have the same function. If a prophet is called to the local church, he may get words for the nation, but that doesn't change the fact that his predominant function and calling rest within the local church. This same concept applies to those who operate in the gift of prophecy, bringing edification, exhortation, and comfort (see 1 Cor. 14:3). When we've been entrusted with a gift, we must never try to turn it into an office unless we've clearly been given that office by the Lord. As we will discuss in the next section, when we try to step outside of our God-given authority, we enter dangerous territory.

As we have seen throughout this book, it is Jesus who sets *some*, not *all* in the fivefold offices of apostle, prophet, evangelist, pastor, and teacher. The spiritual position and authority of these offices has been chosen and set by God. It is not a result of our own choosing, titling, or desired position, but it is the crown of authority we wear in His honor as we represent Him in the earth.

THE THRONE SET IN HEAVEN

The Throne set in Heaven is the place where the authority behind all callings, offices, and ministry functions originates.

> *And immediately I was in the spirit: and, behold, a throne was set in heaven, and one sat on the throne* (Revelation 4:2).

This is what makes what the Lord has crowned us with more powerful and accurate. John saw the One who sat on the Throne—the One who has all authority and delegates it as He desires. The mere fact that the Throne was *set* in Heaven tells us that this is the place from which all power and authority comes and is delegated. Every calling, gifting, and anointing comes from this place of positional authority. Any and all authority, titles, ministry functions, or anointings are given and distributed by the Lord of the Church, as He wills. The apostle Paul mentions this when speaking of the gifts of the Holy Spirit. We don't get to pick and choose which gifts we want, and it's unwise to compare our giftings and callings with others'. God has established the Church with its fivefold offices as His prototype and blueprint to follow here on earth.

> *And God hath **set** some in the church, first apostles, secondarily prophets, thirdly teachers, after that*

miracles, then gifts of healings, helps, governments, diversities of tongues (1 Corinthians 12:28).

The Throne being *set* in Heaven also means we should not, prophetically speaking, try to be a spiritual "ambulance," rushing to every need or crisis that arises, because we may or may not have been delegated the authority needed to address it. Also, we may not have clarity or a word regarding a given situation because the Lord has chosen not to reveal it, or it is out of our spiritual jurisdiction or positional authority. Trouble comes when we try to step outside of the positional authority God has granted us, in efforts to promote ourselves. Another way to think about this would be in the case of a police officer driving outside of their designated patrol area. If they travel to another city or state, they have no jurisdiction to make an arrest because they are outside the territory that's been assigned to them.

This is what Jesus meant when He said some call themselves apostles and they are not.

> *I know thy works, and thy labour, and thy patience, and how thou canst not bear them which are evil; and thou hast tried them which say they are apostles, and are not, and hast found them liars* (Revelation 2:2).

This verse shows us that Jesus is the One who sets them in and determines their gifting and calling, as *He* has chosen. Paul the apostle had to defend his apostleship but also clarified his set positional authority by saying, *"Even though I may not be an apostle to others, surely I am to you! For you are the seal of my apostleship in the Lord"* (1 Cor. 9:2 NIV).

It is dangerous when we step outside of our spiritual "set" place, calling, and positional authority because we can begin to operate outside of the God-given graces and anointings delegated to us. This causes us to be poor representatives of the Throne Room and can lead to our own perspective being communicated on a matter rather than the Lord's. It also can lead to harmful repercussions that have caused some to not finish their race.

One such case of dangerous consequence is Moses' brother Aaron, who stood in a self-appointed "set" place to mislead the children of Israel in Exodus 32. He stepped into a delegated place of authority that was not given him, and as a result there were serious consequences that followed. He stepped in as the leader of the people when it seemed that Moses had delayed in coming down from being with God for several days. This led him to address the people without a "set" mandate and positional authority of God's grace to do so at that time and in that situation. This, of course, led to him creating a false image or perspective. In Aaron's case, it was the image of a golden calf. It might be safe to say that this was not the only unfortunate consequence of taking upon a "set" position not given him; he would also later have his mantle removed, which cost him his very life (see Num. 20:12,24-28). Notice that the removal of his mantle and the loss of his life didn't happen immediately after the incident with the golden calf, and no repercussions or consequences were mentioned at that time. It could have been delayed due to the intercession of his brother Moses.

"And the Lord was very angry with Aaron to have destroyed him: and I prayed for Aaron also the same time" (Deut. 9:20). We must never think that our actions will not or cannot eventually catch up to us when we get outside of the grace God has given us.

This is why we must never treat the holy callings, giftings, and anointings without a deep respect, honor, and fear and not deviate from what God has called us to. We must not pressure ourselves or expect prophetic ministers to always have a prophetic word, revelation, or insight for anything that demands an answer. Prophetic ministers may get people who write and ask them to address an issue, crisis, or event that has happened in the earth. For example, an earthquake happens in a certain place or a tragedy happens in another and people will ask, "What is God saying?" The prophet may or may not be given spiritual insight or authority by Heaven to address it. Remember, even genuine prophets and those who prophesy don't know everything that happens in the earth! We even find Elisha, one of the most gifted prophets in history, asking a question to the Shunammite woman, to whom he had prophesied. He'd told her that she would have a child but now the child is dying. Though he was a prophet, he didn't know that this was what happened when the boy's mother came to seek him.

> *So she went and came unto the man of God to mount Carmel. And it came to pass, when the man of God saw her afar off, that he said to Gehazi his servant, Behold, yonder is that Shunammite: run*

now, I pray thee, to meet her, and say unto her, Is it well with thee? is it well with thy husband? is it well with the child? And she answered, It is well (2 Kings 4:25-26).

Staying within your set spiritual authority and assignments is important. We find this in Luke 4 with the prophets Elijah and Elisha. Notice that there were many needs, but these prophets were only sent to meet one of them as their specific assignment at that time.

I assure you that there were many widows in Israel in Elijah's time, when the sky was shut for three and a half years and there was a severe famine throughout the land. Yet Elijah was not sent to any of them, but to a widow in Zarephath in the region of Sidon. And there were many in Israel with leprosy in the time of Elisha the prophet, yet not one of them was cleansed—only Naaman the Syrian (Luke 4:25-27).

They stayed in their set spiritual jurisdiction, assignment, and authority and were more effective because they did so! This is the mark of a mature Throne Room prophet or vessel. It is usually easy to spot an immature vessel when they know everything about everybody. They always seem to know what is going on in the church, even more so than the pastor. That is dangerous, especially if they always seem to say that God showed them something before He showed the pastor or anybody else. You will be a much better Throne Room representative with greater accuracy when you stay in your spiritual authority and let God increase it and address any issue at hand.

I remember when the Lord told me to close my Bible at the end of one of my messages and end the service. I could feel the pull in the room from the people for me to flow in personal prophecy and to prophesy over everyone in the room. He said, "I want this to train you and those in this service. It is to teach you to stay in your spiritual assignment given and for others to learn to discern the anointing present for this particular setting." As I walked off the stage, I knew in my heart I was doing what the Lord wanted, but I continued to sense a pull from the people and felt like I was disappointing them. At the same time, I felt their disapproval, but the Lord was stressing to me the importance of closely following His leading, regardless of other people's expectations.

While I am not against someone being led to prophesy by the Holy Spirit, it's important that we stay in the assignment the Lord has given us. This is due to knowing the spiritual assignment and responsibility given. We must become disciplined in our set spiritual assignments from the Throne Room and not just do things because that is what is being asked of or expected of us. That may be the call and assignment of others or prophetic presbyteries, but make sure you know if it is yours and when you should do so. I have often been asked to prophesy by request after a service, at conferences, and in other settings. We are to always respect and honor the One who called us and whom we represent, first and foremost. There may be times we feel to minister to those who request, but every prophet needs to be given the space to decline. We must not go against our spiritual assignment given and set from within the Throne Room.

WHAT DID YOU COME OUT TO SEE?

But what went ye out for to see? A prophet? yea, I say unto you, and more than a prophet (Matthew 11:9).

In Matthew 11:9, we see Jesus questioning people in reference to John the Baptist, who was a prophet. Why was He asking them these questions? He was saying that all vessels and giftings must avoid the need to perform for others. This is especially true in the prophetic—that we not allow people to pull us into prophesying or ministering at their desire or request. As those who desire to genuinely represent the Throne Room, we must always avoid the need to perform.

Jesus asked, "What did you come out to see?" This is one of the dangers of the prophetic and what may cause a genuine prophetic minister to miss it. It is the feeling of the need to perform—to see or hear something "new" or "powerful" because people are watching. This performance trap is easy to fall into when our eyes are on ourselves or others rather than on the Lord. But we must never forget the One whom we serve and represent. He is far more important than fame, status, recognition, or approval.

Remember, the Throne Room prophet Jeremiah was told by God to not be moved by people's faces, meaning not to be swayed by their reactions. *"Be not afraid of their faces: for I am with thee to deliver thee, saith the Lord"* (Jer. 1:8). When you are not moved by others' faces or looking for their approval, you won't feel the need to change your words in order to get a positive response from them. At the same time, we are not to let people's *negative* responses, criticisms, or opinions hinder us in revealing what God has told us to speak.

When we are seeking the approval of man, it can cause us to also seek promotion from man, rather than from the Lord. We must be wise not to allow others to promote our giftings or push us into areas or prophetic unctions that God hasn't given. Remember, promotion comes from the Lord. *"For promotion cometh neither from the east, nor from the west, nor from the south"* (Ps. 75:6). It purposely doesn't mention the north, as that is the direction of Heaven, the place of all promotion. We see this mentioned in Isaiah 14:13, when Lucifer wanted to exalt his throne *"above the stars of God...in the sides of the north."*

Jesus references the importance of avoiding self-promotion in Luke 14, in the illustration of the banquet. He says when you are invited, don't be quick to seat yourself up front where everyone can recognize you and acknowledge you; don't promote yourself but rather let the host, speaking of God, promote you. Otherwise, if you are moved from the place you were not invited or promoted to, others will see it and cause you to embarrass yourself and misrepresent the host.

Avoiding performance and self-promotion is a great self-examination that helps in our proper representation of the Throne Room. The apostle Paul encouraged us to examine ourselves and know our true motives. Now, he is not talking about self-condemnation or self-critiquing that leads to criticism and a negative view of ourselves. Self-examination will cause us to look at things like knowing how to properly behave in the house of God.

> But if I tarry long, that thou mayest know how thou oughtest to behave thyself in the house of God, which is the church of the living God, the pillar and ground of the truth (1 Timothy 3:15).

Another area of self-examination is to make sure we are avoiding immaturity and carelessness. Remember, this is why the face of the man is important, as we mentioned previously. When we present ourselves correctly, our giftings, anointings, and ministries will be better received.

> Let no man despise thy youth; but be thou an example of the believers, in word, in conversation, in charity, in spirit, in faith, in purity (1 Timothy 4:12).

We must avoid unnecessary antics or things that would move people away from you and the words you carry. When Paul said, "Let no man despise your youth," he was essentially saying, "Don't act immature." How might someone ministering in the prophetic act immature? Immaturity is often revealed in how a person acts when their prophecy or gifting isn't noticed or received. It can manifest through temper tantrums, rude behavior, creating a scene or generally being in need of a sit-down and a "timeout," where they receive spiritual input and correction. When Paul said, *"let all things be done in decently and order,"* he was speaking as an apostolic overseer and father of a church full of believers ministering in spiritual gifts (1 Cor. 14:40). There had to be an order and a decency in how they presented themselves as well as their giftings.

When ministering in spiritual gifts, it is wise to learn what is right and what is wrong in how we represent the Throne Room, ourselves, and the words we've received from the Lord. A great example is Nathan the prophet, who is allowed to speak to King David regarding his adultery with Bathsheba (see 2 Sam. 12). Did Nathan handle his leader correctly? We find that he did, by speaking his prophecy in a story that was honoring to David while at the same time revealing his sin and need for repentance. Nathan didn't speak with disrespect or in a self-promoting way to prove he was a prophet with an accurate gifting. He handled the king correctly and in order. It was not his place to correct the king, no matter how powerful his gifting was.

> *Where the word of a king is, there is power: and who may say unto him, What doest thou?* (Ecclesiastes 8:4)

Nathan was given access and positional authority by King David because he was a proven, trusted prophet in both his character and gifting. The same will be true when we represent ourselves correctly with others, treating them with honor and respect, as it will open doors of opportunity to share what the Lord gives us. Nathan spoke the truth in love by telling David a story and allowing it to convict his heart. There was no self-seeking or disrespectful behavior from the prophet. This is perhaps why some are never given the open doors to speak to influential people—they lack proper Throne Room representation in their order and manners.

Let's talk again about the pressure to perform that we can sometimes feel when we're in certain ministry situations. Regardless of the situation, we should never feel pressured to perform, especially if we're around others who seem to have a more prominent gifting or anointing. This is especially true when it comes to receiving words of knowledge.

Receiving words of knowledge is an area where performance and error are widely seen. The supernatural gift of the word of knowledge must be just that—it must be by the Spirit of God with a supernatural release of knowledge you didn't previously have. It is vital that the words we deliver are really coming from the Lord and not our own prior knowledge of something we've seen or heard in the natural. We must never act like we've received information supernaturally when, in fact, we've read it or heard it from the news media, another person, or it's simply our own opinion.

Presenting prior knowledge as the word of the Lord is one thing that causes genuine prophets and prophetic vessels to become false. As we discussed earlier, always let people know if you had prior knowledge of something before you speak a prophetic word. It may be that that prior knowledge sparked a word in you to share. That is fine, but just be sure to communicate that to the person receiving your words. This will uphold your integrity and allow them to hear from the Lord more clearly. This couldn't be more important than in the social media and information age, where we constantly have unlimited information at our fingertips. Again, if God is not moving you to release a word of knowledge, don't feel the pressure to perform. In the same way, if you *are* delivering a word, avoid the pressure to add more specific "details" than what the Lord has given you.

One final thought on this: as prophetic vessels, feeling the need to keep up with the anointing of our last meeting or the last powerful word we spoke is a great goal, but not what should drive us to the point of error where we deliver wrong or false prophecy. This can happen when we feel the need to be more powerful. Stay away from the "what did you come out to see?" pressure or mentality and continue to make Throne Room representation your highest goal and honor. This will help you carry the right spirit and the right words when called upon by the Lord or by others.

THRONE ROOM PROPHETS AND THE GOODNESS OF GOD

As we bring this chapter and book to a close, I want to encourage you with an insight that will aid in the Lord's return but will also help you in your Throne Room anointing, accuracy, and representation. It is the revelation of promoting His goodness. Jesus said that the Gospel of the Kingdom, which is the *good news*, will be preached or promoted, and then the end will come. *"And this gospel of the kingdom shall be preached in all the world for a witness unto all nations; and then shall the end come"* (Matt. 24:14). This is not only the message we need to carry but also the spirit from which we need to prophesy. Jesus displayed this, as the spirit from which He spoke was full of love and goodness, even when He had to speak harsh words, warnings, or rebukes. Wherever He went and whatever He set out to do, His goal was to display God's goodness!

> *How God anointed Jesus of Nazareth with the Holy Ghost and with power: who went about doing good, and healing all that were oppressed of the devil; for God was with him* (Acts 10:38).

Our character, the way we represent Him, and especially what we speak on His behalf must carry the spirit of God's goodness. This is what makes the New Testament prophetic minister unique—the fact that Jesus Christ has injected love into the earth and God's wrath has been satisfied through His Son's death on the Cross. This doesn't mean the Lord doesn't get angry; it means everything He does now is based on what His Son has accomplished. Jesus' sacrifice has opened the way for the Father's goodness to touch every person in the earth throughout history! This is what the angels were singing about when they showed up at the announcement of Christ's birth— God's goodness and kind intention toward us!

> *And suddenly there was with the angel a multitude of the heavenly host praising God, and saying, glory to God in the highest, and on earth peace, good will toward men* (Luke 2:13-14).

This message was from the Father's heart to the shepherds, the people of the earth, and all generations going forward. His message, His Spirit, and His heart have not changed. This doesn't mean we will necessarily have peace between nations or even individuals, but God is saying, "My peace, My wrath has been satisfied through Jesus' shed blood. Therefore, My intention is for you to know I have goodwill toward all men!"

We as prophetic ministers must carry this same message and this same spirit, which is His Spirit, straight from the Throne Room—the message that God is good, and His intention is good toward *all* men. God is desiring good things for all men, even if there needs to be correction or warnings of judgment at times. When words like that are spoken, we need to ask, "What is the message of God's goodness that He is trying to reveal and that will manifest if we obey?"

It is important to the Lord that you understand His goodness. He desires to reveal His goodness that will follow His children all the days of their lives (see Ps. 23). This same goodness will lead the sinner to repentance (see Rom. 2:4). It was so important to God that Moses understood His goodness that it was the first attribute of His character that He described. Notice that God didn't say He'd make all His *wrath* pass before Moses!

> *And he said, I will make all my goodness pass before thee, and I will proclaim the name of the Lord before thee; and will be gracious to whom I will be gracious, and will shew mercy on whom I will shew mercy* (Exodus 33:19).

This spirit and message of His goodness is what separates an Old Testament prophet from the New Testament prophet. The Old Testament prophet had to prophesy without the measure of love that was injected into the earth through Jesus' death and resurrection, because He had not yet come and died for all. This made not only a difference in the earth but a difference in how God dealt with mankind. Because of Jesus' death and resurrection, we now speak from a spirit of love no matter whether it is a word of warning, correction, exhortation, edification, or comfort.

Genuine prophetic vessels understand what was accomplished through Jesus Christ. They speak God's redemptive plan and have a strong revelation of God's goodness, not only for themselves, but for others—regardless of their situation. Again, this doesn't mean the Lord doesn't judge, warn, rebuke, or get angry. And it doesn't mean these prophetic vessels don't speak strong words of warning, correction, or rebuke. It just means the spirit in which they minister and the message they bring always intends to point people to God's goodness and mercy toward them.

When a prophetic vessel doesn't consider His goodness in their prophecies, their spirit and perspectives will deviate from His heart and often carry a negative or harsh spirit.

We see this in Scripture when the twelve spies were sent into the promised land under the direction of God and Moses. Only two, Joshua and Caleb, came back with a good report of God's redemptive plan for them to take out the giants and seize their promised land. There were ten other spies who couldn't see God's goodness or His redemptive plan and came back with doom and gloom prophecies from their negative perspectives and spirits. This hindered the whole nation and kept them from entering the promised land the way God had prophesied they would. In the same way, when prophetic vessels get caught up in the doom, gloom, and evils of the day, they have to be careful not to prophesy only from that position and miss God's goodness or redemptive plan in their midst. This kind of mindset, like the spies', will keep the Body of Christ and the nations from entering into what God has planned. Sure, there may be hardships, giants, and challenging times, but like Joshua and Caleb we must have a different spirit that can see God's goodness and redemptive plan from the Throne Room and promote it in the earth.

When the Lord is truly speaking a word, there will always be the element of God's goodness attached to it. Again, we always have to ask ourselves what spirit is speaking. Jesus addressed this with James and John, whom He renamed the Sons of Thunder (anger) because of their short tempers. These two disciples were hotheads and were known for forgetting God's goodness, having the wrong perspective, and speaking from the wrong spirit.

> *And when his disciples James and John saw this, they said, Lord, wilt thou that we command fire to come down from heaven, and consume them, even as Elias did? But he turned, and rebuked them, and said, Ye know not what manner of spirit ye are of* (Luke 9:54-55).

Did you see that? They wanted to call down fire upon these people! Jesus' rebuke shows us that they didn't see the good the people were doing for the Lord and, thus, got into the wrong spirit. This is what happens to all prophetic vessels if they forget the goodness and mercy of God.

Unfortunately, some in the prophetic ministry never recover from being negative and fear-based and prophesying doom and gloom without God's kindness and redemptive plan attached. This is due to spending most of their time calling out what is wrong with something or someone or viewing life through the lens of negativity. It is important to remember that one who is feeling the need to call down fire, rebuke, warn, or declare judgment from God could very well be speaking out of a skewed perspective.

A word of this kind should only be delivered if a person has a healthy understanding of God's goodness and redemptive plan. Any word of rebuke or warning must come from the right spirit of God's intention to extend kindness and mercy to a nation or people. It must also be delivered in the right spirit, with the pure motive of restoration and redemption, and the speaker must be led by the Holy Spirit on how and when to deliver such a word. Yes, God is a God of warnings and judgment—but always remember, vengeance is the Lord's and not ours (see Rom. 12:19). Mercy always triumphs over judgment (see James 2:13).

When a prophetic vessel wants to take on the persona of an Old Testament prophet or perhaps wants to appear powerful or have the latest, greatest prophecies, they begin to go down the road of error. They get into a wrong spirit, mindset, and message by assuming their prophecies have to sound harsh and judgmental to appear powerful and God-inspired. We find these types of prophecies are usually missing the elements of God's goodness and consistent accuracy.

As we can see with James and John, it wasn't an evil spirit they were speaking from but their own anger and their own spirits. Jesus corrected them, as He will do for all prophetic vessels who choose to stay close to Him. It should be the Spirit of the Lord, who is good, speaking through our spirit and promoting His goodness throughout the earth.

When one is given to always seeing the negative in things and the pronouncing of God's anger and judgments, they may be operating from a wrong spirit due to their own fear or lack of understanding of God's goodness. Other times, as we've discussed throughout this book, they can speak from a wrong source, agreeing with the spirit of the culture rather than carrying the Spirit of what God is saying in the midst of the season. As we've mentioned, those who tap into the wrong realm can yield to a wrong spirit, perspective, and open themselves to an evil spirit that can bring fear and even divination with it.

Let's go back for a moment, to the coals of fire that touched Isaiah's lips and Ezekiel eating the scroll that tasted like honey, as they are both reminders of how we can be Throne Room representatives of His goodness. Like Isaiah, when we have been set on fire by the Lord and our words carry the very burnings of His heart, we won't be like James and John, wanting to call down fire from heaven on others. And like Ezekiel, our words need to carry the taste of Heaven's honey or Heaven's sweetness, even if they include correction or warning. Let's always be sure that we deliver words in the Spirit of power, love, and soundness.

I encourage you to covet to prophesy, but as you do remember that the four faces that we've talked about must be our image as well. We want all four faces represented well in us so that our words promote the goodness of God. Remember to stand bold as the lion, humble as the ox, honorable as the man, and to soar in your prophetic gifting like the eagle. You are His voice, sharing His heart, and promoting His goodness as you prophesy.

> If I speak in the tongues of men or of angels, but do not have love, I am only a resounding gong or a clanging cymbal. If I have the gift of prophecy and can fathom all mysteries and all knowledge, and if I have a faith that can move mountains, but do not have love, I am nothing. If I give all I possess to the poor and give over my body to hardship that I may boast, but do not have love, I gain nothing (1 Corinthians 13:1-3 NIV).

Scripture tells us to do everything in the spirit of love. Love is the foundation of all the beauty, majesty, and holiness we see in the Throne Room. Love is the One who is seated on the Throne, and as we pursue the things we can only find when we "come up higher," we are really pursuing Love Himself. It is a tremendous honor to be entrusted with the thoughts and plans of the Lord's heart from the Throne Room. May we be willing to pay the price, whatever it might look like, to properly convey God's heart of love to the world. And may the words we speak ring true in the hearts of men, carrying the power that brings healing and redemption throughout the earth!

About

HANK KUNNEMAN

Hank Kunneman pastors Lord of Hosts Church in Omaha, Nebraska, with his wife, Brenda. Together they host a weekly program, *New Level with Hank and Brenda,* on Daystar Television Network. As an author and uncompromising voice for God's Word, he is known for a strong prophetic anointing, preaching, and ministering in meetings and on national television programs. His ministry has truly been marked for accuracy in national and worldwide events.

Printed in the USA
CPSIA information can be obtained
at www.ICGtesting.com
LVHW050757011123
762208LV00007B/133